Women Matter
The Why and How of Gender Diversity
In Financial Services

Daralee Barbera, CFP CMFC CLF ChFC
Thomasina Skipper, M.B.A., ChFC CLU CLF
Linda Witham, CFP ChFC FIC

Vivia - Best wishes for a meaningful career at a fantastic company - Thrivent! You will change many lives.

Linda Witham

i

WFW Publishing, a division of Walking FilmWorks, Inc. wfwpublishing.com
ISBN-13: 978-0-9970988-1-5
WFW Publishing, Manhattan Beach, CA

To contact the authors, please send an e-mail to women_matter@icloud.com or call (714) 474-8226.

Dedication

Daralee Barbera:

To my wonderful parents, who provided me, and my dear siblings, with an open window to the world, with support to create and find our own path. To my husband, Laurence, whose love, creativity, and inspiration encourage me daily. To my children, Desirae and Gianni, my son-in-law and daughters-in-law, stepsons, and grandchildren, of whom I am so very proud.

Thomasina Skipper:

I stand on the shoulders of all of the women in my family who have come before me and stand with me. My mother was committed to education as a means to a brighter future for her four daughters. My grandmothers worked so very hard to make their families' lives better. My older sisters supported and loved me through all my quirks. To my daughters, daughter-in-law, and granddaughters, I hope my journey helps you fight the good fight to be heard and recognized! My husband, son, and son-in-law are examples of strong men not threatened by strong women. I dedicate this book and the message it brings to women and men so that we can make a difference!

Linda Witham:

To my father, who taught me humility, grace, and forgiveness and assured me that I could do anything I put my mind to.

To my mother, who taught me determination and persistence.

To my husband, Dave, who supports, encourages, and challenges me with his adventurous spirit and zest for life.

Table of Contents

Foreword

It is no secret that it is critical to the profession that we attract more women to the business as advisors, and it is even more critical to move them into management and to retain them in those positions. What women bring to the table is a unique perspective that can actually expand the industry by attracting more female clients and by serving all clients in a more robust way. In turn, women's presence in our firms and agencies can enhance people's financial security for people globally.

It's not necessarily about men versus women, or women as a niche market or a demographic. It's even beyond inclusion—it's actually about *expansion*. This profession offers so much that falls in line with what women are looking for, both as advisors and managers. If we can crack the code of attraction as we move forward, it will be the key to the sustainability of the industry.

I am excited about this book, *Women Matter*, because it is exactly the type of resource the industry needs to achieve this critical expansion. This book is refreshing because it takes a deep dive and an insightful look into how to attract more women to the career.

To ensure that our firms and agencies mirror our marketplace, I think it is going to take a huge wave of professional development about the benefits of hiring more women. It's going to take an intentional effort by the industry as a whole to recognize and acknowledge that women are different—how we sell to women, how we recruit women. It is not a one-size-fits-all environment.

Because this territory is unfamiliar to a lot of people, I think there is a mentality of fear surrounding our ability to move forward. We need to educate people about the potential that lies in what they can be embracing. We are going to have to become intentional about the need for gender diversity and the opportunity that's out there. I think the opportunity hasn't been sold properly to a lot of managers yet. They are selling themselves short by not looking at it themselves and embracing the concept.

It has taken a while to convince some managers that women are viable advisors and managers. I think they finally believe it, but they don't know what to do with it. That is why resources like *Women Matter* can be extremely helpful—to give managers a jump-start and mind-set change as we chart these blue oceans. I don't think people are being stubborn or willful about not embracing this issue; I just think they don't know where to start.

Gender diversity is one of the five key pillars in GAMA International's new strategic plan. We are being extremely intentional about committing the time and the resources to make this a priority. GAMA looks at it from a two-prong perspective.

First, GAMA wants to create an environment in which you have a wonderful experience as a GAMA member. We want you to have an *enhanced* experience based on your demographic. If you are a multiline person, we want you to derive value from sharing best practices with other multiline members. If you are in your first five years of management, we want you to have a positive new-manager experience. If you are a woman, we want you to be able to thrive as a woman in this industry and connect with other women.

GAMA is working to create a robust women's program that is for women, mentored by women, and supports women. We want to create a mentoring relationship, a peer-networking opportunity for them so that they can share their challenges and successes.

The second prong to this effort is that GAMA is taking on a new initiative to educate and professionally develop managers so that they understand the opportunity that exists with women within this industry. We want to educate managers about how to recruit women. It's not about who the manager is; it's about what the manager needs to know.

Whether you ae black, white, Hispanic, male, female, or transgender, you need to be given the tools and resources to understand what you need to be aware of when you're talking to a woman. What might attract a woman to this career? And what should you pay attention to if you want to talk to your female agent or advisor about moving into management? Once she is promoted, then what are the roles and responsibilities of the home office, the General Agent, and the Managing Partner in supporting her? In many cases, this support is different for women than it is for men.

The game has changed, and we need to be mindful of certain things now. In *Women Matter,* the three highly respected authors make a compelling case for the fact that expanding your sales force to include more women can increase your revenues significantly. They also provide the insightful, practical "how to" strategies that they learned the way we all have to learn—through trial and error, successes and setbacks, and hard-earned experience. I hope you will make gender diversity a priority in your organization.

—**Bonnie Godsman,** CEO
GAMA International

Acknowledgments

Daralee Barbera:

My thanks to the many financial services industry leaders who contributed to this book and provided invaluable support for our project. Working together is the way to make progress on any worthy initiative, of which this is truly one. As we are the sum of the parts, I acknowledge the collective contributions and inspiration of colleagues, friends, and family, whose collaboration and sharing have helped make this book a reality.

Thomasina Skipper:

I have to acknowledge my husband, Benjamin Skipper, for always being my bedrock of unrelenting support and encouragement. When it was not popular in the early nineties, he willingly quit his job to follow my dream! He agreed to be the stay-at-home parent and raise our children while I worked my way up the corporate ladder. Without him, I could not have achieved any success. He was there to hear my stories of success, failure, discrimination, hostile work environments, and unfair playing fields. He would also tell me how much he believed in me and trusted me and that he thought I could do anything! He would shower me with his love and send me back out into the world to do what needed to be done.

Linda Witham:

I appreciate the assistance of so many industry leaders who contributed their thoughts as we wrote this book. I want to acknowledge and thank Karsten Lundring, my mentor and co-Managing Partner, who spent the past twenty-five years transforming our organization into a gender-friendly culture. I am forever grateful to my first manager, Louise Evenson, who became my role model for a professional woman leader in this industry.

About the Industry Leaders We Interviewed

We wanted to capture the insight, wisdom, and perspective of women who have achieved top leadership positions in the insurance and financial services industry. The more voices that contribute to this call for leadership, the stronger the call becomes.

We applaud the following women for their achievements and are grateful for their time and contributions to this book:

Susan L. Combs, PPACA, President, Combs & Company, New York, New York

Susan L. Combs, the person, also happens to be the past president of Women in Insurance & Financial Services (WIFS). Susan established Combs & Company, a full-service insurance brokerage firm, when she was only twenty-six years old. She and her team have "a flair with the mundane and expertise in the weird and unusual." Her company specializes in serving niche markets in areas such as entertainment, food-based businesses, and international companies that are expanding their operations into the United States. In 2014–15, Susan served as the president of WIFS and was the youngest national president in the organization's eight-decade history.

Diane Dixon, CLU, Owner, 3F Coaching, Xenia, Ohio

Diane is the owner of 3F Coaching, a national coaching business providing dynamic business planning, life planning, and accountability to profitable entrepreneurs, small business owners, teams, sales professionals, and individuals who want to live a "larger" life.

She worked in the financial services industry for more than thirty years and is a national past president of WIFS. In 2008, she was named the WIFS Woman of the Year. She is a graduate of Coach University, a member of the International Coach Federation (ICF), an affiliate of The One Page Business Plan™, and a practitioner with Leading From Your Strengths™.

Diane is the coauthor, with Charlie Reed, of the 2015 book *Financial Services: Women at the Top—A WIFS Research Study*.

Lily Fong, M.B.A., CLU ChFC CASL RICP, Vice President of Business Development, AIG Partners Group, Nashville, Tennessee

In her current role, Lily is responsible for channel growth and distribution while cultivating and penetrating new business alliances to generate new revenue and meet the needs of a changing market. A native of Hong Kong, Lily chairs the International Committee for GAMA International. In 2013, GAMA named her its Volunteer of the Year. In 2013, Lily received the International Leadership Foundation's Leadership Award. In 2007, she was named one of "50 Outstanding Asian Americans in Business."

Juli McNeely, CFP CLU LUTCF; Owner and President, McNeely Financial Services, Spencer, Wisconsin

In 2014, Juli became the first woman to serve as the president of the National Association of Insurance and Financial Advisors (NAIFA) in the organization's 125-year history. She is the author of *No Necktie Needed: A Woman's Guide to Success in Financial Services*.

Juli joined her current agency, which her father founded, in 1996. She specializes in retirement planning, education funding, business continuity planning, and estate planning. Her clientele consists of business owners, individuals, married couples, and successful professionals.

Juli was named the 2015 WIFS Woman of the Year. She is a frequent speaker at industry events and has been interviewed by many media outlets, including *The Wall Street Journal*, Reuters, *InvestmentNews*, the *Atlanta Business Journal*, *Employee Benefit Adviser*, *InsuranceNewsNet*, and *National Underwriter*.

Stacy L. Nystrom, M.B.A., Partner and Recruiter, Thrivent Financial, St. Paul, Minnesota

As a partner with Thrivent, Stacy is in a field leadership role and helps lead a regional financial office. She is an active recruiter and guides her team of financial representatives to success by coaching and training them to be a valuable resource to strengthen Christian communities. She has been with Thrivent for nineteen years. Previously, she served Thrivent as a Senior Marketing Strategist and a Senior Investment Product Manager.

Arthea Staeger (Charlie) Reed, Ph.D., CLTC, Financial Representative, Northwestern Mutual, Asheville, North Carolina

Charlie is a senior financial representative with Northwestern Mutual and senior partner of Long Term Care Insurance Connection. She was formerly a professor and chair of the Education Department at the University of North Carolina–Asheville (UNCA). She earned a doctorate at Florida State University and is a UNCA professor emeritus. She entered the financial services industry in 1996. She is the coauthor, with Diane Dixon, of the 2015 book *Financial Services: Women at the Top—A WIFS Research Study*.

Emily Viner, Vice President of Agency Growth & Development, The Guardian Life Insurance Company of America, Greater New York City Area

Emily joined Guardian in 1998 after starting her career in the field. A passionate advocate for the career and mentor to many, Emily was responsible for creating Guardian's strategy to attract, develop, and advance women in distribution. Between launching the strategy in 2013 and year end 2015, Guardian has seen a 71 percent increase in the number of women in leadership roles. Emily's goal is to ensure the growth of field leadership and to once and for all create gender balance in financial services. Emily was the 2015 recipient of GAMA International's Cy Pick Award, and in 2009 she was named the WIFS Woman of the Year.

Jocelyn D. Wright, M.B.A., CFP; State Farm Chair for Women and Financial Services; Assistant Professor of Women's Studies, The American College, Bryn Mawr, Pennsylvania

Jocelyn serves a dual role in her position at The American College. She is the director and chief ambassador in leveraging research and education to create broad awareness of the challenges and opportunities that pertain to women and financial services. She is also responsible for the course FA 204: Marketing Financial Services to Women and contributes material on women's issues for other courses offered at The College. In addition, Jocelyn is the founder and Managing Partner of The Ascension Group. As an advisor since 2002, she partners with her clients to design a personalized holistic strategy to help them reach their financial goals.

Also, at LAMP 2015, two of the authors of this book, Thomasina Skipper and Linda Witham, interviewed industry leaders about their views on gender diversity in our industry. We have compiled the responses from these interviews in the Appendix of this book. These are the industry leaders we interviewed:

Sherry Bogus, Branch Sales Manager
Bankers Life & Casualty Co.
Houston, Texas

R. Michael Condrey, CFP CLU ChFC CASL, Managing Partner
Dee Condrey, Recruiter
Northwestern Mutual
Raleigh, North Carolina

Sheri Cooper, CLF FIC CLTC, Managing Partner
Thrivent Financial
Fargo, North Dakota

Ed Deutschlander, CLU CLF, CEO, North Star Resource Group
Mary Anne Smith, Second Vice President, Securian Financial Network
Diane (Dee) Yohn, CLU RHU FLMI CLF, Executive Vice President, North Star Resource Group
Davin J. Bell, Financial Advisor, North Star Resource Group
Minneapolis, Minnesota

Herman Dixon, M.B.A., CLU CLF CPC ELI-MP, Energy Leadership Business Coach, Speaker, and Trainer
Charleston, South Carolina

Sandra Hughes, M.B.A., ChFC CLU, Agency Management
State Farm Insurance Companies
Madison, Wisconsin

Henrietta Nye, Owner
Keir Educational Services; Coach; Trainer
Cincinnati, Ohio

INTRODUCTION:
Why This Book Is Worth Your Time

"Every company, organization, or group with the ability to inspire starts with a person or small group of people who were inspired to do something bigger than themselves. Gaining clarity of why, ironically, is not the hard part. It is the discipline to trust one's gut, to stay true to one's purpose, cause, or beliefs. Remaining completely in balance and authentic is the most difficult part."
—Simon Sinek, *Start with Why*

Why Should You Care about Gender Diversity in Your Agency or Firm?

In the hectic day-to-day busy-ness of a field leader's world, it is difficult—but essential—to pause when considering any new or reengineered strategy and ask, *"Why* should we/must we implement this strategy?"

You may already be convinced of the "why" in your focus on agency/firm gender diversity. If that is the case, you can speed-read the statistics in Chapter 1. We suspect you will still find the research to be fascinating, and you may have some statistics of your own to add to the current research. If this is an initiative you are committed to, you will want to articulate clearly the vision for gender diversity in the agency, firm, or company you serve, if you haven't already. And you will want to envision the expected outcomes so you can measure your progress toward your goal. If you are already doing all of this, we applaud you.

One agency crafted its "why" this way:

> The agency envisions an organization that reflects the gender diversity of the marketplace we serve in order that we may make a lasting difference in the lives of our clients and thereby grow our firm by X percent over the next five years.

You will find other ideas for crafting your agency vision statement in Chapter 2.

In his book *Start with Why*, Simon Sinek says, "Very few people or companies can clearly articulate *why* they do *what* they do. By *why* I mean your purpose, cause, or belief—*why* does your company exist? *Why* do you get out of bed every morning? And *why* should anyone care? People don't buy *what* you do; they buy *why* you do it."[1]

If our answer to that question is "to provide optimal service to our clients to change their lives and help them manage their financial resources," then we can do that best if our firms and agencies mirror the marketplaces we serve.

---

1   Simon Sinek, *Start with Why: How Great Leaders Inspire Everyone to Take Action* (New York: Portfolio/Penguin, 2011), 39.

Why We Wrote This Book

We wrote this book to provide *specific strategies* to any leader in the financial services industry who wants to have an organization that (1) reflects the demographics of the people it serves and (2) will be successful in the new generation. It is a call for leadership (not for management).

Tim Schmidt, a Managing Partner with Thrivent Financial, talks about the three I's: inform, inspire, and ignite. That is what we want to do with this book. We want to inform readers about why gender diversity is critical, inspire the industry's leadership to take action, and ignite a desire in leaders to use our strategies and make a positive change.

I (Linda) originally got the passion for writing this book about a year and a half ago at a LAMP meeting (GAMA International's annual conference). I was sitting there thinking that even though it was 2014 at the time, there was still a lack of sensitivity among many male managers in our industry about how to communicate with women and, more importantly, a lack of understanding about *how* to recruit, train, and support women. I realized that, to give our industry hope, what we need, especially for middle managers, is a guidebook that will help them avoid repeating the mistakes of their elders and actually make a difference in the gender diversity of our industry.

Throughout this book, we weave our own experiences from one hundred collective years as female producers, frontline managers, and agency/firm first-line leaders.

And then, in an attempt to make it more broad-based and also to have more fun doing it, I thought, "Why do this alone? Why not reach out to two of my best friends, whom I really respect, and who can very justifiably represent a different segment of the industry than I do?" That is why I reached out to Daralee and Thomasina and asked if they wanted to do this together.

Throughout this book, we weave our own experiences from one hundred collective years as female producers, frontline managers, and agency/firm first-line leaders. Writing this book as a team is just one more example of the way women approach projects—collaboratively.

Research Proves the Benefits of Gender Diversity

If you are picking up this book out of curiosity and wondering why there is such hullabaloo about gender diversity in our industry, you will want to spend time digesting the research summarized in Chapter 1. We hope you will take the time to understand the implications for our industry and for the organization you serve. You will see that having women on your team can increase your organization's profitability, enrich relationships with clients, and attract younger people, including Millennials, to your sales force.

With this book, it is not our intent to create new research because excellent sources of data are already available from many reliable sources, including LIMRA, the GAMA Foundation, and The American College. In addition to the research in Chapter 1, we have referenced many original sources for your further study in the back of this book.

After a study of the research, we believe you will understand the *why* of gender diversity.

Then you will be ready to draft your agency or firm's gender-diversity vision statement, which we discuss in Chapter 2. *Do not underestimate the importance of a clearly defined vision.* We believe the clarity that a vision statement brings to an initiative has been one of the missing links in our industry's struggle over the past several decades to achieve gender diversity.

Those two chapters compose Section 1, "The State of Our Industry." In Section 2, "Practical How-To's," are ten chapters to give you specific ideas you can implement to achieve gender diversity. We gathered these tactics from our own experience and from other industry leaders in gender diversity.

We believe the clarity that a vision statement brings to an initiative has been one of the missing links in our industry's struggle over the past several decades to achieve gender diversity.

It's Time to Pass the Baton

Rome is burning. Today, the average first-line leader in our industry is in his or her sixties. Already the reins are being handed over to the next generation of leaders. This is our unique opportunity to finally take a stand and help this next generation of leaders avoid going down the same self-defeating path of exclusivity the older generation did. We care about our industry because we care about the people we serve. But if we do not change our direction, we are about to see our industry be less and less effective.

Simple things are keeping many male managers from having a gender-diverse group. They use poor language and make assumptions. They make the culture of the organization still feel like an old white boys' club. Because I (Linda) am a forgiving spirit, I would like to believe that they are not doing it out of malice but out of ignorance and a lack of awareness.

I (Thomasina) am not as forgiving as Linda. I am mad as hell, and I don't want to take it anymore. I believe we have been too kind and too generous to the folks in power and waiting for them to eventually come around to do the right thing. I think they will never come around to do the right thing unless they have a real reason. And those reasons are becoming more profound every day, to the point where I am beginning to fear for our industry.

We are slow to address the changing demographics. In the United States, women represent almost 60 percent of annual university graduates and more than 70 percent of 2012 high school valedictorians. Women account for 60 percent of master's degrees and more than half of doctorates being awarded in this country. More than 52 percent of college graduates are women, and more than 50 percent of doctors and lawyers are women.[2] We are the people who are supposed to serve female professionals, yet our firms and industries do not mirror our new marketplace.

This is a serious topic that needs urgent attention. To work to increase awareness is not only the right thing to do; it is also a wise business decision with great economic merit. About 51 percent, or $14 trillion, of American personal wealth is now controlled by women, according to the Bank of Montreal's Wealth Institute. The Canadian bank also expects

---

2   Joseph Chamie, "Women More Educated than Men But Still Paid Less," March 6, 2014, YaleGlobal Online, Yale University website, http://yaleglobal.yale.edu/content/women-more-educated-men-still-paid-less-men.

women to control about $22 trillion by 2020.[3] Plus, on average, women live longer than men. We need to provide service in a way that enables women to accomplish their financial goals and objectives. We need to start with the end in mind, which, again, is the critical "why" question—"*Why* are we all here?" The answer is to be of service and to positively impact as many lives as possible— and that includes women.

The Main Reason People and Companies Change

I (Thomasina) believe that people don't typically change because they *want* to. Usually they change because they *have* to—and this is a "have to" situation. We ought to be shouting loudly that this is our industry and we love it and that the future of this industry is embracing gender diversity. I believe that is the linchpin to everything else. We need to knock down the door and represent the population, which is 50 percent women. If 50 percent of the people in our industry and in our leadership are women, then I believe younger people will have a better culture to come into. Young folks are not willing to accept what the old, white-male regime is putting forward. That is why companies are having problems recruiting the best and brightest to our industry.

> *Young folks are not willing to accept what the old, white-male regime is putting forward.*

In 1975, a woman named Muriel Kraszewski sued State Farm Insurance Companies when she filed a sex-discrimination complaint with the Equal Employment Opportunity Commission. She joined State Farm in 1963 and worked for the company for twelve years at an annual salary of $8,000. She did much of the high-level work for her bosses, who each earned about eight times her salary. When she asked to be promoted to agent, her request was denied because she did not have a college degree— even though few of the managers had degrees.

In 1988, Kraszewski won the lawsuit and $431,000. And in 1992, State Farm paid a $157 million settlement. At the time, it was the largest damage recovery in any case brought under the Civil Rights Act of 1964. More importantly, the lawsuit motivated State Farm to greatly step up its goals for hiring women.[4]

I (Thomasina) got hired in 1986 as a result of that lawsuit. The company was forced to change, and today it is gender-diverse. When I retired in 2013, 50 percent of the managers on my regional team were female. If you walk through our home office in Bloomington, Illinois, you will see that it is the most diverse environment in the industry. The company employs women, African Americans, Latinos, and Asians.

When I went into management in 1992, I was told that I could not hire a white male until I hired a female or a minority. As a manager, I remember one meeting where I was the only African American female at the table. My Agency Director went around the room and asked all the managers, "Where are your women? Where is your diversity?

3   Ryan Gorman, "Women Now Control More than Half of US Personal Wealth, Which 'Will Only Increase in Years to Come,'" April 7, 2015, Business Inside website, http://www.businessinsider.com/women-now-control-more-than-half-of-us-personal-wealth-2015-4.

4   Adam Bryant, "The Woman Who Sued State Farm and Won," April 30, 1992, *The New York Times* website, http://www.nytimes.com/1992/04/30/business/business-people-the-woman-who-sued-state-farm-and-won.html.

All the guys replied, "We can't find women candidates anywhere."

When they asked me, I said, "I can't find a white man to save my life."

The reason? Human nature. We tend to gravitate toward, and hire, people just like us. As a result, our agencies and firms end up looking just like us, not like our marketplace. When I walk into a room and see that there are twenty people in the room, and they are all white males except for one African American female in the corner, guess where I am going to go? I am going to go sit with her. That is human nature. We have to understand that and break the cycle. And we have to do it for a reason bigger than what is comfortable. That is what we are asking—for people to step out of their comfort zones because something really good is going to come out of it.

Dare to be different. Be one of the leaders who changes because you want to, not because you have to.

Diversity Isn't Just about Gender

The focus of this book is gender diversity, but it's important for us all to keep in mind that if our firms and agencies are to truly mirror our marketplace, we need to achieve diversity in race, ethnicity, age, and other areas as well.

We also need to recruit people with disabilities. People with disabilities and other perceived "disadvantages" may surprise you with an unbreakable determination to succeed. I (Daralee) have had the privilege of working with such top-producing, successful advisors. These inspirational individuals are examples of viable candidates who could have been potentially overlooked. Preconceptions and bias regarding what a financial professional looks like are often narrow and obsolete. It is time to replace that image with a broad and inclusive visual that reflects our clients.

Emily Viner, Vice President of Agency Growth & Development for Guardian in New York City, believes a focus on gender diversity can pave the way to other types of diversity:

> Gender is the highest level of diversity. If you have an environment with more women, I think that the culture shifts, and you tend to attract other diverse groups and people with different thinking than your own. By creating environments where both men and women thrive, we've taken one step toward inclusion. And after that first step, you're on a path that better enables you to be inclusive of other groups that are underrepresented in our industry. It changes the environment and the conversation. I think it makes an organization more interesting to more people.
>
> It is a natural progression to being a completely diverse and inclusive organization, and that can only help the American public by providing choice and diversity of thought. Recently a coach was talking about one of our General Agents who moved from Minnesota to Dallas to take over an office. He said, "Just go to the best mall in Dallas and walk around for a day. That is what your office has to look like." It is common sense, but in the past, we as an industry have not done a good job of reflecting the population.

Achieving diversity in our organizations will often require stepping outside of comfort zones, providing an important opportunity for personal growth. It will take more work for some leaders than others, but we assure you it will be worth the effort.

Let's begin the exciting and rewarding journey to creating a more diverse industry. Why? Because women matter.

Questions to Ask Yourself

1. What percentage of the marketplace you serve is composed of women, people of diverse races and ethnicities, and people with disabilities?

2. What percentage of the people in your organization represent those populations?

3. If your organization does not mirror the marketplace you serve, what has prevented you from achieving diversity in the past?

4. What are some practical steps you have taken to change the demographic makeup of your organization to date, and what have your results been so far?

5. What timeline will you commit to, right now, for achieving measurable results in this area?

The Why:
The State of Our Industry

CHAPTER 1

The Research and Our Purpose Give Us the "Why"

"I always valued men and women equally, and I found that because others did not, good women economists were cheaper than men. Hiring women does two things: it gives us better-quality work for less money, and it raises the market value of women."
—Alan Greenspan, American Economist and Chairman of the Federal Reserve of the United States, 1987–2006

The monumental question of "why" looms before all of us—*why* should we spend time, effort, and resources trying to attract more women into our industry?

1. **The business case for hiring more women**—From a practical standpoint, as we mentioned in the introduction, it makes sense for any business to mirror the marketplace it serves. You are more likely to attract a diverse client base if your sales team is diverse—and that means you will have a much bigger pool of potential clients. Also, because so few agencies and firms excel in this area, your organization will stand tall above the rest if you make gender diversity one of your goals. Women matter to your bottom line.

2. **The unique strengths women contribute to an organization**—Ample research suggests that women enhance teams and organizations in ways that men cannot. This means your teams can be more effective, you will be able to serve clients in a more robust way, and everyone in your firm or agency will see client service from a broad new perspective.

3. **Our purpose**—Given our role in the community, we can help women enhance the quality of their lives by educating them about financial management. Because women tend to respond better to female advisors, we can reach more female clients if we add female advisors to our teams.

These reasons all contribute to your bottom line. If your teams are more effective and women help you serve more clients in a more thorough manner, that will boost your bottom line. Likewise, if you hire women to help more women learn how to become financially secure, that will enhance your professional reputation and trust in the community, which also will boost your bottom line. There are many compelling reasons to embrace gender diversity.

Let's look at these three answers to the "why" question in more detail.

The Business Case for Hiring More Women

The way many firms and agencies do business still aligns with the way things were done in the 1960s, when men were the primary income earners and managed the household finances. Times have changed drastically. These statistics from a 2015 report by the GAMA Foundation show the significant impact and influence women have in the United States:

- Women now compose 51 percent of the US population and 47 percent of the labor force.

- Since 2006, women have earned more than half of bachelor's degrees (57 percent), master's degrees (60 percent), and doctorate degrees (51 percent) in this country.

- As of 2014, the United States had nearly 9.1 million women-owned businesses, which account for 30 percent of all privately held firms. Between 1997 and 2014, the number of women-owned firms grew at 1.5 times the national average.

- In the United States, women currently control 50 percent of the private wealth and head one out of three households.

- More than nine out of 10 women (93 percent) polled by Insights in Marketing reported having a significant influence on the financial services their family purchases. The same survey revealed that a similar percentage of women (87 percent) would like to work with a financial advisor—but only 17 percent actually do.[5]

Here are some additional eye-opening statistics to consider:

- In the United States, women exercise decision-making control over $11.2 trillion. That represents 39 percent of the nation's estimated $28.6 trillion of investable assets. And nearly half of that amount—$5.1 trillion—is managed solely by women.[6]

- According to a 2013 Insured Retirement Institute study, 70 percent of women seeking advisors say they would prefer to work with a woman.[7]

- According to the Bureau of Labor Statistics, in 2013, 25.7 percent of personal financial advisors were women.[8]

5 "Recruiting Women to the Advisor Career," GAMA Foundation for Education & Research, 2014, p. vii.
6 Sylvia Ann Hewlett and Andrea Turner Moffitt with Melinda Marshall, "Harnessing the Power of the Purse: Female Investors and Global Opportunities for Growth," 2014, Center for Talent Innovation, http://sister-scapital.com/wp-content/uploads/2014/05/HarnessingThePowerOfThePurse_ExecSumm-CTI-CONFI-DENTIAL.pdf.
7 Jennifer Barrett, "Why Do Advisors Have Such a Hard Time Reaching Women?" February 2, 2015, CNBC website, http://www.cnbc.com/2015/02/02/sors-have-such-a-hard-time-reaching-women.html.
8 "Household Annual Data Averages," Bureau of Labor Statistics website, http://www.bls.gov/cps/cpsaat11.pdf.

These numbers tell us that the women are out there, and they are educated, financially savvy, involved in financial decisions, and want to work with female advisors. These statistics are incredible, yet our industry is ignoring them. Women are influencing buying decisions—not just for groceries and clothing, but for major purchases like homes, cars, and financial investments. Yet these staggering statistics have not resonated with many managers in our industry. The facts have not made any marked difference in our behavior. Our actions need to reflect the reality of the facts.

Bersin by Deloitte just released a study revealing compelling evidence that inclusion pays off. Over a two-year period, the company surveyed and interviewed more than 450 global companies to identify their level of maturity in a wide variety of talent practices. Researchers looked at 128 different aspects of talent management, such as how well companies assess candidates for job and culture fit. Then they looked at those companies' business performance. The two areas that correlated with the highest impact on business performance are all about inclusion and diversity.

"Inclusion is the goal we want to achieve here, and diversity is the measure of success," says Josh Bersin, the company's principal and founder. "The fact that diversity and inclusion rated the highest impact of all points out that in today's working world, your ability to attract and engage people of all ages, cultures, backgrounds, and types is paramount to your business success."[9]

Unique Strengths Women Bring to Your Firm or Agency

Women make teams more effective.

Women and men have different communication styles (see Chapter 5). Women tend to be more patient and communicative, and they tend to look at a client's overall financial situation over time rather than immediate performance of a portfolio. That approach resonates with many people, especially women, and helps build long-term client relationships that are based on trust and mutual respect.

Here are other reasons why women can be an asset to your firm, agency, or company:

1. **Women make teams more effective**—Professors at Carnegie Mellon, MIT, and Union College found that teams with more women outperformed teams with more men. It was not "diversity" (having equal numbers of men and women) that mattered for a team's intelligence, but simply having more women. The reason, in part, is that women, on average, are better at "mind reading" than men. In other words, women were better at "reading" other people's emotions, both in online and face-to-face interactions.[10]

2. **Women are better at multitasking**—In 2013, researchers at the University of

---

9   Josh Bersin, "Why Diversity and Inclusion Will Be a Top Priority for 2016," December 6, 2015, LinkedIn, https://www.linkedin.com/pulse/building-diversity-inclusion-op-priority-2016-josh-bersin.

10   Anita Woolley, Thomas W. Malone, and Christopher F. Chabris, "Why Some Teams Are Smarter than Others," January 16, 2015, *The New York Times* website, http://www.nytimes.com/2015/01/18/opinion/sunday/why-some-teams-are-smarter-than-others.html?_r=0.

Pennsylvania found striking differences in the way men's and women's brains are wired. The differences may explain why, on average, men are better at learning and performing single tasks, such as cycling or navigating, while women tend to be better at multitasking and problem solving in group situations.[11]

3. **Women are often better managers**—Catalyst, a nonprofit that promotes women in business, found that over the course of five years, companies with women on their boards had average returns on equity of 15.3 percent, while those of companies without any female board members were 10.5 percent. (Return on equity is a figure that indicates a company's ability to generate profit from shareholders' investments.)[12]

Women matter to your organization because they contribute to the client experience in ways that men cannot.

Our Purpose: To Guide Women in Building Financially Strong Families

So we know that women are influential in financial decisions, want to work with female financial advisors, and control much of the country's wealth. By failing to hire female advisors, we are missing a significant opportunity to help women realize their financial dreams and protect themselves and their families from the financial risks associated with early death, disability, and sickness.

I (Thomasina) think the humanity aspect of hiring women to this career—our purpose—goes very deep. Women do control a significant amount of wealth in this country, but women also make up the biggest sector of poverty in the United States. When women are financially savvy and work so that they're able to take care of their kids, the kids stay out of trouble and out of jail. The parents have better jobs and live in better places. It is important to the health of our society that we have women doing meaningful work making a good income. If women keep making only 77 cents on the dollar and they are heads of households, then we don't have financially strong households.

There is a difference between income and wealth in this country. Many women will make the same income as men but not get to a position of wealth. The American College has studied what women do with their income. They help their kids and other relatives. Daughters will impoverish themselves for the sake of their aging and sick parents, while some wealthy sons contribute little or nothing toward their care. Women start out making less, and then we make different choices with our money than men do. We start out in a hole, and then we keep digging.

But when you get into a career like this, it teaches you how to handle money, how to invest money, how to feel differently about money, and how to help other people with their money so that they don't go out and spend $100 on a pair of kid's tennis shoes because they don't know that they should be putting it someplace else. Most young people, especially

---

11   Catharine Paddock, PhD, "Brain 'Wired Differently' in Men and Women," December 4, 2013, *Medical News Today* website, http://www.medicalnewstoday.com/articles/269652.php.

12   Joe Pinsker, "Hedge Funds Run by Women Outperform Those Run by Men," August 4, 2014, *The Atlantic* website, http://www.catalyst.org/system/files/the_bottom_line_corporate_performance_and_women's_representation_on_boards_%282004-2008%29.pdf.

girls, do not learn how to manage their finances. If your parents didn't teach you, chances are, you didn't learn much about it. No one has ever had a discussion with most women about long-range planning. Many women don't believe they can ever buy a house. We can show them how they can buy a house, support their families, and send their kids to better schools. Knowledge can change a woman's socioeconomic status and her ability to move the next generation to a better place. If we get this right, we can make a major impact on society as a whole.

If we get this right, we can make a major impact on society as a whole.

As leaders in this industry, we are the guardians of the standards set in the industry. We help people create and manage wealth. There are so many women out there whom we are not working with. We could help change their lives for the better if we would just get more involved. Our industry has a huge opportunity to educate both men and women about financial stewardship. Educating people will make our communities stronger. When tragedies occur in the lives of these women, our work with them will not remove the grief, but we can relieve the financial burden because of the work we do.

It is this passion for helping others and making a difference in their lives that drives us to hire women advisors who can best serve the women in our communities.

Why Many Managers Are Reluctant to Hire Women

The reasons to hire women are overwhelmingly positive. So why haven't we hired more female advisors and managers?

Many of the obstacles are related to the vestiges of the past—biases that have hung on through the decades. These biases aren't always intentional, but they are detrimental anyway.

Sadly, female managers are often just as reluctant as male managers to hire women in this industry and to promote them into management. So we are not pointing the finger at male managers; this is something we all need to remedy. Here are some common obstacles that keep women from entering our industry.

1. **There is a general bias against women**—In 2013, three academic researchers discovered a hard-wired bias against hiring women for positions that require a knowledge of mathematics, despite their ability to perform just as well as men with numbers. Three researchers found that *both male and female hiring managers* were one and a half times more likely to hire a man than a woman. One reason: in interviews, women tend to be self-effacing about their abilities, while men often brag.[13]

2. **Opportunities are often given to those who conform to masculine stereotypes**—Research by Catalyst found that talent management systems are frequently vulnerable to pro-male biases that result in less diverse employee pools. This is because senior leadership teams, which tend to be dominated by men, set the tone for talent management norms, so masculine stereotypes can creep into HR selection tools. Employees are selected for promotion and/or tapped as future

---

13 Dan Cook, "Managers Show Bias against Hiring Women," March 28, 2014, BenefitsPro website, http://www.benefitspro.com/2014/03/28/managers-show-bias-against-hiring-women.

leaders and/or offered development opportunities only if they meet criteria that are potentially based on masculine stereotypes. Because male-dominated industries and occupations tend to be particularly vulnerable to masculine stereotypes due to lack of diversity, women may find it particularly difficult to excel in these industries or occupations.[14]

3. **The age-old "double standard" prevails**—A November 2014 Pew study found that about four in ten Americans think women are underrepresented in leadership positions because of a "double standard for women seeking to climb to the highest levels of either politics or business, where they have to do more than their male counterparts to prove themselves." About the same number of Americans say the electorate and corporate America are just not ready to put more women in top leadership positions.[15]

4. **Many managers are reluctant to hire women of child-bearing age**—One of the most common barriers to hiring women is a prevailing attitude among many managers that it's expensive and inconvenient to hire women who are of child-bearing age. They cite the cost of maternity leave and the hassles associated with having to replace the female employee while she is out on maternity leave and the fear that she might not return after having her baby. But some studies show that this logic is unfounded. For example, after California instituted paid medical leave, a 2011 survey by the Center for Economic and Policy Research found that 91 percent of employers said the policy either boosted profits or had no effect. They also noted improved productivity, higher morale, and reduced turnover.[16]

Susan Wojcicki was Google's first employee to go on maternity leave when the startup launched its operations in her garage in 1999. When Google increased paid maternity leave from twelve weeks to eighteen weeks in 2007, Wojcicki says the rate at which new moms left Google fell by 50 percent. (The company also increased paternity leave from seven weeks to twelve weeks because of the positive effect it has on families and the business.) She says, "Mothers were able to take the time they needed to bond with their babies and return to their jobs feeling confident and ready. And it's much better for Google's bottom line—to avoid costly turnover and to retain the valued expertise, skills, and perspective of our employees who are mothers."[17]

Is there a single reason *not* to make your firm, agency, or company more inclusive? We don't think so. Everyone can benefit if you hire more women—you, the other people in your organization, the women you employ, your clients and prospects, and the entire

---

14 Anika K. Warren, "Cascading Gender Biases, Compounding Effects: An Assessment of Talent Management Systems," 2009, Catalyst website, http://www.catalyst.org/system/files/Cascading_Gender_Biases_Compounding_Effects_An_Assessment_of_Talent_Management_Systems.pdf.

15 "Women and Leadership: Public Says Women Are Equally Qualified, But Barriers Persist," January 14, 2015, Pew Research Center website, http://www.pewsocialtrends.org/2015/01/14/women-and-leadership/.

16 Susan Wojcicki, "Paid Maternity Leave Is Good for Business," December 16, 2014, *The Wall Street Journal* website, http://www.wsj.com/articles/susan-wojcicki-paid-maternity-leave-is-good-for-business-1418773756.

17 Ibid.

community you serve. Be a gender-diversity trailblazer, and become the role model for other field leaders to emulate.

Questions to Ask Yourself

1. In this chapter, we have presented many reasons why gender diversity is a wise business decision. Which of the reasons resonate most with you personally?

2. Think about women you know and admire. What unique strengths do they contribute to a team effort? Which of their strengths could benefit your firm or agency?

3. Do certain members of your management team have or voice biases against women? If so, what will your strategy be to overcome those biases?

4. Put some numbers on paper. Given the demographic makeup of the communities you serve, if you could attract 20 percent more female clients in one year, how quickly would your revenues cover the cost of hiring more women?

CHAPTER 2

Envision It, Commit to It, Make It Happen

"The secret of achievement is to hold a picture of a successful outcome in mind."

—Henry David Thoreau

A high-net-worth woman walks into your firm or agency. What does she see? We said earlier that 70 percent of women prefer to work with female advisors. How many female advisors can she choose from if she decides to work with your organization? What if she were to ask you, "Why do you have so few female advisors?" How would you respond? Would you become embarrassed or defensive, or would you make up an excuse for why you have so few? Or would you say this: "We are working on it. In fact, our goal is to have half of our agency composed of women in three years."

We know that women control the majority of the wealth, and the majority of the clients we serve are women. So *what* do you want that woman to see when she walks in your door? Does your firm have a culture, an environment, she can relate to? Does she feel comfortable reading a magazine and sipping a cup of tea while she waits for her advisor? If half of your advisors were women, what would that look like in your organization? Take a moment to picture it. Envisioning it will make it easier for you to make it a believable aspiration.

Take the First Three Steps to Make It Happen

Here are three key steps to take in achieving gender diversity:

1. **Commit to making gender diversity a focus in your firm, agency, or company.** In Chapter 1, we talked about the "why." Your *why* has to be compelling enough to give you the incentive to commit to making it happen.

2. **Put that commitment in writing, and share it with everyone in the organization.** It needs to be communicated so clearly and so often that if someone walked around and asked anyone who works for you what your commitment to hiring women is, they will all be able to repeat your goal, objective, or vision.

3. **Create a detailed plan.** Specify how you will reach your goal, year by year, department by department, unit by unit.

So *what* do you hope to accomplish in the next year? The next three years? Five years? The next ten? *How* will you accomplish it? We want to challenge you to commit to ambitious goals. Those goals must be stated within a specific time frame, realistic given your current resources, and tied to profitability. This will require some number crunching on your part. Here is an example of a gender-diversity vision statement:

Sample Vision Statement

Within the next two years, we will recruit, select, train, and develop twelve women to represent and mirror the demographic segments of our marketplace.

When I (Daralee) create my annual business plan for recruiting every year, I include a statement about diversity. I make it a deliberate focus so that everybody else reading my business plan knows it is important.

Set Ambitious But Realistic Goals

Obviously, this is an initiative that takes time. We recognize that recruiting, selecting, training, and developing new recruits are processes that require a lot of resources.

For example, let's say you are a middle manager whose unit is composed of 20 advisors—18 men and 2 women. To get to a 50/50 balance, you need to keep your 18 male advisors and eventually have 18 female advisors. You already have 2, so you need to hire 16 women. But you can't hire 16 in a year because you probably can't train 16. Let's say you can hire and train 6 new advisors in one year.

So you hire 6 women. Now you have 18 men and 8 women, and almost 31 percent of your advisors are women. If you hire 6 additional women the next year, then (assuming you have no attrition), you'll have 18 men and 14 women; now almost 44 percent of your advisors are women. You're close to having a 50/50 balance, and it took only two years. The more underrepresented women are in your firm or agency, obviously, the longer it will take you to achieve diversity. But the sooner you begin, the sooner your advisor force will mirror your market and bring significant new opportunities to your advisors and your organization.

Please be careful about letting your view of what is and is not realistic slow your progress.

Please be careful about letting your view of what is and is *not* realistic slow your progress. I (Thomasina) have seen too many cases in which we have said to folks, "We don't expect you to get to 50 percent in one or two years. We are going to let you slow walk." Well, a slow walk turns into a slow drag, and that's why we are here, with only 26 percent of all advisors in this country being women. In all the years I have managed people, I have seen that the lower the goal a manager sets, the worse the actual success is. Let's aspire to doing something bigger and better. Aspire to hire women.

Let's say you have 100 advisors, and 3 percent of them (3 advisors) are currently women. You double that number, so now 6 of your advisors are women. It's not time to pat yourself on the back just yet. That isn't nearly enough women to mirror your marketplace. Again, we encourage you to set ambitious goals!

Let's validate the struggles that are inherent in this process, but not allow ourselves to succumb to excuses and to put forth anything less than our optimum effort.

Three Types of Potential Pushback

We realize that a commitment to gender diversity will represent a significant change for many managers. We're not saying it will be easy, necessarily, but we all agree that the effort will benefit everyone involved.

Despite the benefits, though, we envision three main types of pushback to gender diversity.

The "Can't Do It" Manager

The first type of pushback we envision is the manager who does not believe he or she can achieve gender diversity given current resources in the firm or agency. It may require some out-of-the-box thinking about existing recruiting, selecting, and training processes, which we cover in upcoming chapters.

If you can hire and train only six people a year, maybe you need to think differently about how you hire and train.

If you can hire and train only six people a year, maybe you need to think differently about how you hire and train. Maybe you need to have advisors work in teams. Maybe you need to do something different than your normal routine to get past hiring six women a year, to get you to your goal faster, quicker, and more efficiently. It's possible that your current processes will not support this type of initiative. If that is the case, meet with your best people and do some brainstorming about what can be changed in your strategies to reach your goal.

The "Rush It and Ruin It" Manager

A second type of pushback we envision is at the other end of the spectrum. That's when an energetic manager says, "Okay, I am going to hire women only. I am going to go all out and hire ten in the next year instead of my normal six per year." So he lowers his standards to get a lot of candidates in the door quickly. And, because he is in such a rush, he doesn't put in place a plan for how to support and develop female advisors effectively, so they feel out of place and uncomfortable. They quit, and the manager says, "Well, they didn't do very well, and most of them left. See? I knew it wouldn't work. I wasted all those resources. I'm not going to do that again."

We don't want to see anyone on that death spiral, which I (Linda) think some people have experienced. I think that is one reason why our industry hasn't been very successful in hiring women. They take a goal and try to reach it by using the same old process they have used in the past, then wonder why it doesn't work. Your vision must include new processes and strategies to accommodate this new focus.

When I (Thomasina) first got in the industry, I called it the "self-fulfilling prophecy." The men would say, "You know, women can't do well here. African Americans can't do well here." They would go out and hire terrible candidates who didn't do well, and then they would pat themselves on the back and say, "See? I told you they wouldn't do well."

What do we do when another goal in our plan is not met? Do we abandon the goal as unrealistic or not relevant? Certainly not! If our life insurance sales goal is not met this year, we buckle down, analyze the reasons, and revise our strategy to reach it next year.

The "Not on Board" Manager

The third type of pushback is the manager who just won't buy in to the new vision the Managing Director has defined. So what happens if you make the commitment to achieve gender diversity in your organization, but some of your key managers won't support it?

In my (Linda's) experience, any manager in this industry has to deal with change management. The change may involve a process, a goal, or the makeup of your leadership team. In any good change-management process, the first thing you do is try to be empathetic with the person who is having a difficult time accepting the new path forward. Then you try to expand that person's vision of what the future will look like. We think this book can help.

You can give managers assignments and encourage them to become educated on this topic. Have them read the GAMA Foundation eBrief we mention several times in this book. If that person is still resistant to your new vision for the agency, then you have to let him or her go. At that point, it is probably time to take a stand and say, "You are not going to be part of our agency vision, so you are not part of the leadership team."

They have to grow, or they have to go. It takes leadership commitment to make these difficult choices.

People often confuse standards with values, and that causes them to resist certain initiatives. One time, a male manager told me (Thomasina) that he wasn't going to hire a lady because she had gone through a divorce and allowed her husband to take the children. Because of that, he had decided she wasn't a good person, according to his value scale. Sometimes we need to separate our personal value system from our professional objectives. You can still have a personal set of standards without imposing your personal beliefs on your firm or agency.

> *The clearer you are about your intentions, the easier it will be to execute them.*

Can you just imagine what is going to happen in the next ten years as male managers who don't agree with hiring women are hopping around from one company to the next, trying to avoid the tsunami of women coming into the industry? This change is inevitable.

If you write down your vision, goals, and objectives related to gender diversity and communicate them often, it will make it easier to identify anyone who is not on board with your vision. The clearer you are about your intentions, the easier it will be to execute them.

It Doesn't Stop at Recruiting

Once you make the commitment to hiring women, your entire operation has to support their success—it doesn't stop at recruiting. Your training, development, support structure, and culture all have to support gender diversity. The way you approach all aspects of management and leadership must reflect your commitment to gender diversity.

Generally, in my experience as a leader, I (Daralee) have found that it is important to keep the same high standards you have always had, but recognize that you might have to make some adaptations—in scheduling, for example. Sometimes women and men who have young children need flexibility in their schedule. You are not lowering your standards if you change an 8:00 a.m. meeting to 9:30 a.m., or invite parents of young children to participate in the meeting from home. Conference calling and WebEx enable effective remote access.

Don't try to apply your old process to the new reality.

Be creative and adaptable with your process. Don't try to apply your old process to the new reality.

Of all the industries, ours is the most fertile field for the growth of gender diversity because we have a service-oriented mind-set. We want to be of service to our clients; that is what attracted us to this industry. So we can catch up. It will take some work, but it will be well worth the time and effort.

Questions to Ask Yourself

1. How many advisors work in your organization? How many are women? So what percentage of your advisors are women? How many women would you need to recruit to have an advisor pool composed of 50 percent men and 50 percent women? How many new advisors are you able to train each year with your existing resources? Given those numbers, when would you be able to reach a goal of an equally balanced (male and female) advisor pool?

2. In what venues (e.g., meetings, e-mail blasts, newsletters) will you communicate your newly revised vision to ensure that everyone in your firm or agency knows it well?

3. Once you make the commitment to achieving gender diversity, what types of pushback do you envision, and from whom? What will you do about it if it does happen?

The How:
Practical How-To's

CHAPTER 3

Potholes in the Agency's Road to Gender Diversity–And Strategies for Overcoming Them

"I'm not telling women to be like men. I'm telling us to evaluate what men and women do in the workforce and at home without the gender bias."

—Sheryl Sandberg
CEO, Facebook

You have become committed to a gender-diverse organization. You have worked with and/or collaborated with your leadership team to articulate your organization's vision, along with metrics to measure your progress. The leadership buys into the vision.

What will prevent the vision from being achieved? What potholes are in the road ahead that could throw you off course? No doubt there will be surprise obstacles that neither you nor this team of authors can anticipate. Isn't this the norm for an agency leader's world, the "stuff" that keeps our work "interesting"?

In this chapter, we have compiled a list of hurdles many agency leaders have already experienced. Our goal in sharing these potholes—and strategies for overcoming them—is to learn from each other.

Pothole #1: Advisors or Managers Who Don't Buy In

Some advisors and/or managers will object to your gender-diversity initiative. Some might approach you privately and sheepishly voice concern that if you hire more women, "Things just won't be the same around here, and standards will be lower." Be thankful for the relationship of trust you have with these people because they took the risk of telling you how they really feel. The private conversations you have with the skeptics give you the opportunity to enhance those relationships by understanding their fear and coaching them to another place.

> *The private conversations you have with the skeptics give you the opportunity to enhance those relationships.*

Of course, others who have similar fears won't say a word to you. Instead, they will try to sabotage the plan, starting by stirring up water-cooler conversation: "Well, I hear that we're going to have some sort of quota system around here now." This sort of sabotage is, of course, more difficult to overcome.

Strategy to overcome:

Knowing that some people will have these concerns, you will want to carefully manage this change in advance. Just as you would handle any change management, you will need to identify agents/advisors who will most need a personal conversation with you in advance to convey specific information. When you reach out to them in advance of the "general announcement," you are letting them know that you have thought about them and that you are aware of their feelings and concerns. This special attention will go a long way toward getting them on board with your new vision for gender diversity. Make it clear in this early conversation that you will not tolerate "sabotage" talk from any advisor or manager.

Pothole #2: A Rush to Increase the Number of Women Candidates

Your recruiters and frontline leaders rush to source women candidates and lower standards so they can recruit as many they can, as quickly as possible.

This is one mistake many of us have made over the past years, and the result has set the industry back many years.

In our enthusiasm to recruit women, we painted a picture of complete flexibility (instead of managed flexibility) and attracted some women who viewed this career as a part-time job to try out from 9:00 a.m. to 3:00 p.m. while "the kids are at school." Then, when these "part-timers" failed, everyone openly or secretly said, "See? This isn't a career for women with children."

Strategy to overcome:

Take extra care in your selection of the first group of women you recruit. Should you have higher standards for women than for men you recruit? No! Of course not.

The best strategy for high standards is, and will always be, to increase the candidate pool from which you select advisors. Of course, this begs the question of where you find potential candidates. See Pothole #3 on this topic.

In your efforts to increase your number of women recruits, don't paint any unrealistic pictures of the challenges of this career—especially the dedication needed to get one's career started. Women candidates want to know the honest reality of this career. I (Linda) would tell candidates that no matter how many interviews and tests we give candidates, the person who knows the candidate best is that candidate. Therefore, my job in the selection process is to make sure the candidate is fully aware of both the benefits and the challenges she will face. See Chapter 7 for more selection ideas.

Women candidates want to know the honest reality of this career.

Recruit women who will set the standard you envision for your gender-diverse team.

Pothole #3: The Claim That It Is Difficult to Recruit Women to This Career

Your recruiters and frontline leaders say they "find very few women candidates."

One agency leader said, "For the life of me, I just can't find any qualified women." A study of the agency's recruiting sources was revealing. College football coaches and businessmen were the primary centers of influence they relied on to refer potential candidates to the agency.

Many of the women candidates did not test well, and those who had moderate scores didn't complete the selection process. Why? Well, the recruiting brochures pictured male agents and touted income figures for first-year agents who worked sixty to seventy hours per week. The recruiting process included interviews with male agents who emphasized how many "cold calls" they made to get started in their first year. One question in the leader interview was "What are your favorite sports?"

Strategies to overcome:

1. Reevaluate your recruiting sources. Brainstorm new sources that will naturally lead to more women candidates in your recruiting pool. See Chapter 6 for ideas for where source women candidates.

> *Brainstorm new sources that will naturally lead to more women candidates in your recruiting pool.*

2. Reexamine all of your recruiting materials and your entire selection process. Ask other women professionals who are not in this industry for their candid feedback on the gender "slant" that might be embedded in your recruiting and selecting process.

3. Be sure women candidates have informational interviews with successful women agents. "Borrow" these successful women agents from another firm if you don't have any yet.

Pothole #4: Frustrated Female Agents Quitting

Scenario 1: The first female agents quit after less than a year, even though she had achieved a successful start.

Scenario 2: A successful female agent in her second year comes into your office to resign. She sadly explains, "My husband is tired of not having me home in the evening for dinner."

Scenario 3: A successful fifth-year female agent leaves to join another agency/firm. In her exit interview, she highlights the many contests within your agency that offer rewards of fishing trips or baseball tickets. Neither appeals to her.

Scenario 4: In an exit interview, one female agent says, "I always felt singled out as different when I was here. I was never 'one of the guys' because I didn't discuss the football scores at lunch on Monday. The other agents would be cracking up over some joke, and if I walked up, they sheepishly said it wasn't a joke 'for a lady's ears.' Whenever a man used a curse word, he'd always look at me and say, 'Excuse my language.'"

Strategies to overcome:

1. Focus on changing the culture of your organization to be more diverse. Perhaps not all the men advisors are football fans, either. Take the lead in discussing a variety of personal interests in addition to sports, such as music events, art, camping, family outings, restaurants in the area, travel, cooking, etc. If jokes are being told in the office that would make another person uncomfortable, you need to have a private conversation with these agents immediately. Constantly ask yourself and your leadership team, "How will the specific action of these agents look and feel to others—both men and women?"

2. In periodic reviews with all agents, include discussions about family/work balance and time management to help agents be home for important family time.

3. Just as with the male agents or advisors in your organization, include the spouses and significant others of women in culture-building events. It is your job to know all the spouses and significant others of both men and women.

4. Think of as many diverse incentives as possible. Constantly ask all of your agents (both women and men) what is motivating to each of them specifically.

Let advisors bring their children into the office outside of regular office hours.

Pothole #5: The Baby in the Office

A female agent in her first year brings her three-month-old son to the office. Two male agents erupt in anger in your office and storm out, vowing to interview with another company that doesn't "have a nursery for an office."

Strategies to overcome:

1. Rethink your position. If we are flexible and adaptable, it is because we are accommodating advisors who have children—it doesn't mean we are changing our culture or running a daycare. In fact, if clients see an advisor come in with her child because she has child-care issues, I don't think that is off-putting to them; instead, they see that we care about our advisors as people, not just as employees who work for us.

2. Spend focused time to help a female advisor plan during her pregnancy. Be clear that you will help provide support and be sure she has a clear, realistic plan in place. Help her call on her support network.

3. Discuss and publish guidelines for child care in advance of this sticky situation.

4. Let advisors bring their children into the office outside of regular office hours, which might be 8:30 a.m. to 5:30 p.m. I (Daralee) used to bring my kids in all the time, at all ages, especially during the unofficial hours. I would keep them busy and contained in my office, and I would get my work done. They were out of the way of others who were also working, or seeing clients. If it helps advisors to get work done that can't be done at home, there is no reason why this can't be part of the culture.

5. Have one central place where all reps post the times and dates of their appointments with clients in the conference room. We (Linda and team) used to do this so that other agents would know when nobody had an appointment, maybe on a particular Friday, so then it was okay to dress more casually or bring in your child if you had some child-care issues that day. But if the whole calendar was full, with lots of clients coming in, then everybody was expected to put on a more "professional" demeanor.

6. This is an opportunity to adjust the office layout to accommodate some private space for young female agents and to have a serious conversation with the agents who were unhappy. Maybe they should go to another company! I (Thomasina) have a small amount of sympathy for their position, but I have more concern for my industry.

7. When I (Thomasina) was an agent, I arranged my office to accommodate my children. When I moved into management, I encouraged my female and male agents to do the same. This industry is a lifestyle; my children are better business owners and employees because of the exposure they received. They never played house but would always play office!

Among the women who Charlie Reed and Diane Dixon interviewed for their book *Financial Services: Women at the Top*, being able to take children to the office was critical. Here is what Charlie says:

These women had to find ways to make their children a part of their work lives, and several of them had nurseries in their offices. They had young children when they were starting out and when they were growing their businesses, and they had to be able to take care of them because they didn't always have other resources. One woman has a number of State Farm agencies in Florida. She has twin boys, and they had a room in her office. She said that none of her clients ever complained about that; in fact, they absolutely loved it. It created a culture in her office of children being welcome. Now her boys are grown up, and she said that to this day, there are people who bring their kids into the office, and it has really been a plus to her business.

Pothole #6: Men's Assumption That Women Can't Close a Sale

Many men think that women don't know how to close a sale and that it is difficult to train women how to sell. They often assume that women should close sales the same way they do and in the same time frame.

Strategies to overcome:

1. Help new women agents develop their personal style to be successful by learning from a variety of mentors, including other women. The truth is that most people—both men and women—have their own unique selling style. I (Linda) once recruited a female agent into a team with three men; the team was very successful. The team

lead had a personality that was flamboyant; he had a style of talking to clients like no one else. No one—not the female agent, not the other male agents—could learn from him as a mentor because nobody could replicate his style. He got away with it because it was his personality, and he was successful, but nobody else could close a sale like he could. Women particularly found it difficult to learn from his style. It is important in the training process to expose new advisors to many styles and consciously help the women advisors develop a style that is both comfortable for them and effective in the sales process.

2. Train women to understand that good "selling" is helping clients achieve their goals. In fact, plenty of women feel like "sales" is a dirty word. They often don't want to use their good influence to pressure a client to buy. They would rather use a caring, empathetic, "I'm doing this for you" sort of style that probably gets the sale closed at a slower pace but with a much more solid basis of trust and understanding. In my (Linda's) experience, the quality of client relationships and the persistency of the business are high among our women advisors because they are caring and empathetic, they have an effective communication style, and they move at a pace that clients are comfortable with. Men witness a woman doing this and say, "She spends too much time with small talk in the beginning of the sales process and just won't move as quickly as the men to ask for the sale. She is a professional visitor without a process, and she says she is not comfortable using our tried-and-true script." Men need to understand a women's timing, and women need to be encouraged through training to use their supportive, influential style to help their clients achieve goals by buying suitable products. We need to train women advisors to understand that we help clients only if we sell them suitable financial products.

Plenty of women feel like "sales" is a dirty word.

I (Linda) can remember vividly training new agents, both men and women, and talking to them about the importance of not thinking of sales in a bad way but instead thinking of sales as a help to people. One day, I went to Nordstrom to buy a new suit for work. The female sales clerk said to me, "Would you like my help in finding a scarf to match?" Yes, she sold me a scarf, but the way she framed it and the way she provided that service made me think of selling as a help. We need to show our agents how important it is to be confident in knowing that selling is the conduit through which we help people. Our industry has featured, in many cases, a negative kind of selling where you get in and sell clients something quickly, before they ask too many questions. And then you don't ever contact them again because they might change their minds. We must get past this stigma.

3. Reconnect women advisors with the passionate purpose that caused them to join this career. This passion should help women focus on the helping aspect of sales.

4. New female advisors tend to ask more questions during the training process. They are trying to learn every small detail, and they will tell you if they are not ready to move on to the next phase. Be sure your training and role-plays support their "need to know" to increase their confidence.

I (Daralee) have observed that we, as women, tend to have a broader range of acceptable procedures and processes than men do when making sales. In my experience, I have frequently seen women who are flexible and accepting of individual styles. People need to give themselves permission to be themselves and not try to be someone else. Each advisor has to make the process his, or her, own and be comfortable with it. Taking the time to establish relationships, and really focus on the qualitative components of the sale so that it can be long lasting, is time well invested. Time is our friend, not our enemy. Some men worry that if the sales cycle isn't quick, the sale has been lost. Women tend not to feel that way and often build a relationship first and make a client second. Men likely will make a client first and develop a relationship as a result.

Each advisor has to make the process his, or her, own and be comfortable with it.

I (Thomasina) have seen a lot of the "my way or the highway" thinking among men. In fact, I have heard some of the industry's most successful leaders say, "If you don't do it my way, you can't stay in this organization." That comes across as autocratic to women, who are more democratic by nature.

Juli McNeely, an accomplished advisor who is the first female to serve as president of NAIFA, explains how she struggled to find her own style when she entered this career:

> When I started this career twenty years ago, everything was really geared toward a man's style. I wanted to quit every day for the first three years. I found myself being very frustrated because my dad is the one who trained me—or tried. He had a very hard sales style, and I knew immediately that it couldn't be my style. It didn't feel comfortable, so I knew it would never be something I would think I could grab onto and find success with because it just felt very foreign to me. So I had to find my own style. Well, thankfully, my mother also was in this industry, although in a different company than my father, and I learned a lot from her. So finding other female role models and discovering your own style helps a producer so that she doesn't feel like she is being forced to do her job in a way that isn't comfortable to her.
>
> Training programs have evolved a lot already, but I think we need to continue to evolve the training programs to be more geared toward helping new advisors find their own style versus forcing them into a style that may not fit their personality or be within their comfort level. Maybe that will help us retain some of the women we do end up recruiting.

Pothole #7: A Dress Code That Is Geared Toward Men

In some organizations, the dress code is specific and geared toward men only, such as "a light blue or white shirt, navy-blue tie, and dark suit." That sends a clear message that women are not included in the culture.

Strategies to overcome:

1. If a dress code is an element of your culture, make sure it is written and communicated in a way that includes women. Remove any language from your dress code that is male-focused, like "suit and tie."

2. Young women advisors particularly may need "fashion advice" to help them transition from collegiate attire to professional attire. Invite a woman from the *Dress for Success* show or a fashion consultant from an upscale department store to host a women's lunch for female advisors.

Susan L. Combs, president of Combs & Company in New York City, offers this candid advice about a dress code for today's firm or agency:

> A lot of people in our industry still require everyone to button up and wear suits. But many of today's business owners are young, and the Millennials want to feel like they are dealing with their peers, so they want to feel like they match them. They want a real-world dress code. Millennials aren't attracted to feeling like they have to dress like their father when they go on appointments.
>
> We always say in our office that we dress for our clients, so if our clients are all wearing suits, we are going to wear suits. If our clients are in a creative firm and they are all wearing jeans, then we are going to wear jeans and a blazer to that meeting. If I walk into a meeting with some of my clients and I'm wearing a suit, they are going to ask, "Oh, do you have a funeral later?"

Millennials aren't attracted to feeling like they have to dress like their father when they go on appointments.

Top advisor Juli McNeely shares a similar experience:

> Regarding the dress code, I feel that we come a long way there as an industry. But again, back twenty years ago when I started, it was different. We were expected to dress in a suit, or in a jacket with a skirt or pants. It was somewhat cookie-cutter, and that is what I think the industry has encouraged. I think the younger generations are going to buck anything that requires them to wear something that they are not absolutely comfortable in. We need to be sensitive to the generational differences.
>
> Everyone's idea of what professional means can be different, but as long as a woman's clothing is not offensive and it looks professional, I think anyone should be allowed to choose the style that fits him or her best. I will give you an example. When I first started in this career, I thought I needed to look very dressed up. I live in rural Wisconsin. I went to do a retirement-plan enrollment for a farm client of ours. And of course I never even thought that I would be meeting these employees in the barn. I came out of there and thought, "Oh, my gosh. I should never wear this kind of suit to a meeting like this again." You have to

look professional, but you also have to dress for the clientele you are going to be seeing. I never did that again.

This is not just about the clothes that we wear, though. It's also true of our sales style and our communication style. Again, I think that the worst thing we can do as an industry is to be cookie-cutter in our approach. So training programs that push someone into a very set and specific way of doing things run the risk of scaring people off if that is not in their comfort zone.

Pothole #8: Women Who Are Obstacles to Other Women's Success

It isn't just men who can try to prevent women from succeeding. As mentioned earlier, other women may be inclined to be obstacles to other women's success as well.

I (Thomasina) once spoke at a workshop at The American College Women's Conference. Later, during lunch, a woman sitting at my table said, "I am just sick and tired of hearing about women. I don't think there is a problem. I used to play basketball; I'm an athlete. I kick butt, and if these women don't want to do it, tough for them."

I said to her, "You do understand that you're standing on my shoulders, right? It was people like me who came first and took a lot of abuse so that you are able to sit here and say what you are saying and not have to deal with what I dealt with fifteen years ago."

Strategies to overcome:

1. Be aware that some women can be just as reluctant as some men to embrace your gender-diversity initiative. Make sure that your communications about this topic are targeted to everyone in your firm or agency—not just the men.

2. Remember that all women are not the same. This should be obvious, and it is true for men as well. The best way to learn what a specific woman thinks is to ask her. Don't make assumptions.

> *Be aware that some women can be just as reluctant as some men to embrace your gender-diversity initiative.*

Pothole #9: Reluctance to Hire Women of Child-Bearing Age

As mentioned earlier, one of the most common reasons men avoid recruiting women is their worry about what happens if the woman becomes pregnant. How long will she need to be out of the office? Will she be able to focus on her work once she returns? Will she return at all or decide to be a stay-at-home mom? If she stays, will her family responsibilities be disruptive to the business?

The truth is, men are just as likely as women to have life situations that require them to take time off. Active-duty military members (both male and female) could be out of the office for extended periods. Many people care for aging parents whose health is failing. And men and women often share child-care duties equally.

Regardless of the individual's personal needs, the point is that as leaders, we need to have a support system in place. We should make it easy for advisors and managers to conduct their business successfully while also juggling their personal and family needs. Our business is, in fact, extremely conducive to this level of flexibility.

In our industry, we still have the same responsibilities, regardless of what is going on in our lives. Our clients are counting on us. Our leadership and advisors are counting on us. The stock market is still going to open and close at the same time; nothing is going to stop because we have something else going on. That is part of living life. So the reason this can be the ideal industry for advisors and leaders who are living their lives is because we don't do this alone. We don't fly solo. We have a very collaborative approach in all that we do. Even if advisors have their own off-site individual offices, we still support them remotely and support their clients. If someone needs to be out of the office, we just have to reroute everything so we are picking up their calls, intercepting the FedEx packages, and placing the trades.

Even if advisors have their own off-site individual offices, we still support them remotely and support their clients.

Advisors often need personal support. From babies being born to all-star softball travel tournaments to children going off to college to parents needing care as they age, advisors can be in need of special accommodations. When these occasions arise, we should make a point of asking, "How may we help you get through this moment?" You never know what will come up in someone's personal life and how it might affect them professionally. But that is the beauty of our industry. Our clients have personal situations arise, and so do we. Part of the attraction of this career is that it is not nine-to-five and allows for living our lives.

This is a *life* thing, not just a career thing. Women don't stop working because they get pregnant. I (Thomasina) have heard men say, "I don't want to hire a woman who is still in her child-bearing years." Let me get this right. You have nine months to plan for her temporary exit, but the guy she is sitting next to has a heart attack on the way to work, and you didn't have any time to plan for that. But you would rather not hire her, as talented as she is? There are so many stereotypes and myths that we just need to debunk.

When I (Linda) was leading new-associate classes, we had younger people—both men and women—who had issues with how to balance this career with family responsibilities. Being sensitive to family responsibilities applies to both men and women. It is essential to help advisors manage this blend.

And you can't assume that a woman will take a lot of time off on maternity leave.

Early in September 2015, Marissa Mayer, Yahoo's forty-year-old CEO, announced that she planned to take just fourteen days of maternity leave in December after the birth of her identical twin girls. Only twenty-five Fortune 500 CEOs are women, and many women were outraged that one of the world's most influential businesswomen would send the message that women need minimal time off for maternity leave. Caroline Fairchild, founding writer of *The Broadsheet*, *Fortune's* daily newsletter on women in business, said the announcement "sends a signal to young female professionals that if you want to take more than two weeks off when you have a kid, perhaps the C-suite isn't for you." She added,

"Culture is set at the top. Mayer...is setting an inflexible culture."[18]

This is a controversial issue. It is easy to see why some women were offended. And Mayer probably has support, resources, and help at home that most women can't afford. Still, it is her decision, and accepting her decision is part of being open-minded, flexible, and accepting of individuals' personal style and choices.

But did Yahoo stop operating for two weeks while Mayer was on maternity leave? No. Their support structure no doubt allowed the company to operate seamlessly in her absence. Similarly, a career in the financial services industry is well suited to accommodate such individual preferences.

Strategies to overcome:

1. Rethink the "time away" issue. Allow flexible scheduling to accommodate people's needs. Expect the same results from everyone, but allow people to get the job done in a way that is comfortable for them.

2. Allow alternative means of communication. A FaceTime or Skype meeting can be just as effective as an in-person meeting. This is how many younger advisors prefer to communicate. The various forms of social media can be effective communications tools too.

3. Connect a woman advisor having her first baby with other women advisors who have young children. They will give her great creative suggestions to help in planning.

Connect a woman advisor having her first baby with other women advisors who have young children.

Anticipating obstacles before they occur can save you a lot of time, effort, and expense. If you can anticipate potential potholes and address them, you are more likely to prevent them from having a negative impact on your gender-diversity program.

Do not allow any obstacles to cause you to abandon your gender-diverse vision. Adapt your strategies, but don't abandon the cause!

Questions to Ask Yourself

1. Which of the nine potholes mentioned in this chapter do you anticipate that you might encounter? Write down a plan of action for addressing each one of them.

2. What are some potholes we didn't mention that might impact the success of your gender-diversity program negatively? Again, write down a plan of action for addressing each one.

---

18 Caroline Fairchild, "How Marissa Mayer's Maternity Decision Affects Young Women—Whether She Likes It or Not," September 2, 2015, LinkedIn, https://www.linkedin.com/pulse/how-marissa-mayers-maternity-decision-affects-young-women-fairchild.

CHAPTER 4

Always Start with Culture: What to Keep, What to Change

"Leaders who embrace diversity and behave inclusively create the kind of culture wherein female advisors and employees come forward with solutions to drive engagement with the female market."

—*Harvard Business Review*, 2014[19]

As you make the commitment to achieve gender diversity in your agency, firm, or company, you will hopefully find that many elements of your culture are conducive to including women. And you will find that you will need to change others. As you analyze your organization in this context, you'll discover which elements to keep and which to change.

Culture trumps strategy. Sometimes leaders are so focused on the strategies that they forget the "why" behind all of it. We can have good intentions about bringing women in, but if our strategies are not connected to our culture in a logical way, our strategies will not be as easy to implement, and they may not be as successful as they could be.

Sometimes leaders are so focused on the strategies that they forget the "why" behind all of it.

A Culture Built on Serving Others

Joe Jordan is one of the financial service industry's most successful leaders, as well as an author and a compelling motivational speaker. He knows we're in this business to help people, and he understands the life-changing value of life insurance based on personal experience. When Joe was only nine months old, his father, a successful attorney, was killed in a car accident. It was 1952, and just days earlier, his father had cashed in his $100,000 life policy. Joe was the youngest of four children, and their mother, a homemaker, then began to work full time as a secretary because they did not receive a death claim. Joe says that growing up in a maternal household gave him a greater insight into issues that woman face.

More than half a century later, when Joe was fifty-four years old, he realized the impact of his dad's life insurance cash-in. He realized that $100,000 was a lot of money back in 1952, and if his family had received it, their lives would have been different.

Joe has been called the "emotivator," and his presentation during the 2004 MDRT

---

19   Hewlett and Turner Moffitt, "The Financial Service Industry's Untapped Market."

conference is a perfect example of why. In a powerfully emotional speech, Joe told the audience his story:

> I want to know, where was the person of significance, the advocate, who could have taken my father, even pushed him up against a wall and said, "Don't you understand you have to have life insurance?" You have to understand what your sacred trust is. You have to overcome your reluctance to make the call. It has to come from the heart to go out and find people like the elderly woman or my mother because you have to protect them...If someone is disrespectful of you or treats you like a used-car salesman...do you know what you tell them? "What I do for a living is protect the innocent when someone dies prematurely. I provide a worry-free retirement that people can't outlive. I protect their assets when they get sick. I provide a legacy when they die. Because I live a life of significance."

In 2013, Joe published a book based on his story titled *Living a Life of Significance*. Now he has built a set of audio and video vignettes with the same name. One of them is titled "Living a Life of Significance: A Woman's Perspective." For this program, Joe and his team interviewed women advisors about how being a professional in the life insurance world has made a significant impact on their lives and on the lives of clients.

Joe says, "One of the segments is quite emotional and really highlights the burden on women for caregiving and the importance of having long-term care. Another is about a woman who was married for more than thirty years and got divorced. She was terrified that she would run out of money. The woman's daughter asked a friend, who was a financial planner, to talk to her mother, and she did. Because of the peace of mind the financial advisor provided the mother, it was the first time in five years that she slept through the night."

The audio program contains thirteen stories told by industry-leading women. They share their personal journeys and client experiences with single mothers, divorced and widowed women, and caregivers. Each story features insights and commentary from Joe.

Joe has seen a shift away from the emotional aspects of what we do toward a more numbers-oriented focus on selling products.

During his forty-plus years in the financial services business, Joe has seen a shift away from the emotional aspects of what we do toward a more numbers-oriented focus on selling products. He challenges advisors and leaders to focus on the emotional side of the business, the positive impact our profession has on our clients, and the difference we can make when we help people manage their finances well.

So what does all of this have to do with culture? Joe explained it to us this way: "If we spend time focusing on the impact we have on others, that is part of our culture. It gives our agents and advisors the courage to get on the phone and prospect because people's willingness to accept rejection is the DNA of our business. So it has to be because of something bigger than you, not just because of you."

Women Matter and Joe's program, *Life of Significance: A Woman's Perspective*, are similar in that they both call for cultural change in financial services. As Thomasina has said, people don't change unless they have to. With the average advisor age in the upper fifties and a crisis of credibility and trustworthiness from the public and regulators, the current culture has not served the industry well. Joe's revelation in his *Life of Significance* franchise is that our business is less about facts and figures and more about creating trusting relationships. Women do that instinctively! *Women Matter* also mentions that there are women in the industry who are also reluctant to hire and promote women. This is an example of a cultural paradigm that needs to be changed. At his 2015 keynote address to the WIFS Annual Conference, Joe referenced the important value that women have in the financial services industry. He mentioned the impact that two emotions—fear and love—can have in our business. Women show up able to navigate the emotions of the moment and well equipped to show clients the care and love needed to understand them and to provide a process and solutions. To this point, Joe quoted Tim Sanders, Chief Solutions Officer at Yahoo!, as saying, "I define love as the selfless promotion of the growth of others."

You can read more about Joe at http://www.josephjordan.com/.

Think about your organization's meetings and its contest and recognition program. Naturally, sales results will be the primary focus; however, are those results expressed as amount of life insurance in force instead of only commission credits earned? Do you recognize the number of clients helped instead of only commission credits earned? At each meeting, do you highlight the personal stories of clients who have benefited from the work of your advisors?

Everything we do as leaders must keep our organizations focused on the help we provide for clients through the products and services we sell them. We make a significant difference in our communities, and women are an important part of that.

It's Time to Change the Rigid Culture

A culture that's built around helping people feels a lot different than a culture that's built around meeting quotas. Of course we have to set and reach quantitative goals to stay in business, but the way we get there does not have to be as rigid as it has been in the past.

Time blocking—the requirement that advisors have to be at meetings at a certain time—is still prevalent in many organizations today. It's an example of a rigid culture that does not appeal to women—or to the newer generation. The requirement to count dials is in that same category; it creates a non-entrepreneurial culture.

> *A culture that's built around helping people feels a lot different than a culture that's built around meeting quotas.*

What drew me (Daralee) to this career was the flexibility it allows. I was able to be a self-disciplined individual and get the job done on my terms and on my schedule. Cold calling was not promoted as the way to get clients. I used other methods for reaching people, such as teaching classes and providing education. I wouldn't want to be a new associate in our industry if you told me that I was going to be required to time-block and make a certain number of dials every week. I would say, "This isn't what I want to do. I want to do financial planning and help people by tailoring products and services to their individual needs." I think that a culture of rigidity is going to chase away a lot of women and Millennials.

Women may or may not do well with cold calling, but if you put us in a room with fifty other women and give us a mission, we may come out with much better and higher-quality leads. Plus, with all of the technology today, our approach needs to be different. We need to adapt to the way things are changing. Let's embrace a new way of recruiting, training, and promoting people. Let's allow them to market differently than we have marketed in the past.

I (Thomasina) think that if our industry continues to have a rigid culture, it is in big trouble—bigger trouble than it was ten or twenty years ago, when we had the major shift from traditional life insurance to financial services. We are in trouble because we are getting farther and farther away from our marketplace, what they look like, and what they demand of us. We are stuck doing it the way it used to be instead of opening up our minds and seeing the way it could be.

𝒜 Culture of Inclusion

I (Daralee) once got an e-mail from a woman I had not met. She was reading the LifeHealthPro article that mentioned the privilege I had of being named one of the top twenty women in insurance. In my narrative, I had said that if anyone ever wanted to talk about what we do, they should contact me. After I received her e-mail, I set up an appointment to talk to her. She wanted to be in this business to make a difference. She had a friend whose husband was an agent. She had asked her friend, "Can I talk to your husband?" The friend said no.

That shocked me. She explained, "He does not like working with women."

So the local agent, her friend's husband, wouldn't talk to her because she was a woman. How many people are out there who have this experience? I would never dream that somebody wouldn't talk to someone just because they are female. There is a critical need for those of us who are in this business to serve as a resource for those considering this as a career path. This woman had done a lot of research on the career and was prepared for our call. She asked solid questions. I referred her to a local manager for follow-up.

> There is a critical need for those of us who are in this business to serve as a resource for those considering this as a career path.

It is possible that the agent just wasn't set up to train a newbie in the business. And sometimes, agents see anybody else entering the field as competition. Either way, he missed an opportunity to consider her as possibly a valuable addition to his team.

If achieving gender diversity is your goal, then the commitment to get there will need to be built into every aspect of your organization, and every person in the organization will need to understand and embrace it. If one of your values is to include people of both genders, then every word you speak—and every word anyone who works with you speaks—will need to reflect that value.

On the spectrum from not inclusive to inclusive, most organizations are somewhere in the middle. Unfortunately, some have been extreme in their unwillingness to welcome people who are different from them. Lily Fong of AIG Partners Group tells this story about an experience she had that changed the way she saw this industry—and this country:

> Some people see me as a little bit aggressive; I am bold because of my personal experience. When I came to this country, I pictured it as the land of dreams, but in reality, it is not. Let me share my real experience with you.
>
> In the late 1990s, I left AT&T and began working in the financial services industry. I was hired to grow the Asian sales force for the company I joined. So I started my multicultural marketing work, and it went very well at the beginning. Then one day, the president and CEO of the life insurance division came to our meeting. He said something that really changed my life: "This is a white-male company. This is a white-male-dominant industry. You, as an Asian woman, should be out." He told me I should not be there.
>
> I replied, "Why don't you fire me?"
>
> After that, I did start looking for a job, and that is why I quit that company. Other than that, it was a great company to work for.
>
> At that moment, he made me realize that the gender and racial issues really exist in this country. When you look around, most of the senior executives are one color and one gender, and nothing else. So whenever I have an opportunity to advocate for or promote my women coworkers, I will do so. I will push them to the peak of their performance. This is my personal agenda, and that is the reason why I am so bold and such an advocate for my people—especially the minority women because I do not want them to have such a horrible experience as I had with that executive. That really changed the whole landscape of my career.

Shared Values Shape Your Culture

When we have an inclusive, diverse culture, some may ask what we have in common. Therefore, it is equally essential to articulate what we share as an organization. Shared values are what bring people together, and they shape your culture. If we are trying to build an organization that embraces individual differences and cares for individuals, then we have to have

Shared values are what bring people together, and they shape your culture.

something that brings us together—and that is having shared values. So how can managers determine what the organization's shared values are?

In 2002, Thrivent became the largest fraternal benefit society in the United States when Aid Association for Lutherans and Lutheran Brotherhood merged. We (Linda and team) had to blend two cultures that were perceived to be different. One of our first steps was to have everybody look at a list of fifty values and then rank and prioritize their top ten values. Then we all narrowed our lists down to five, and we posted everyone's top five values to see what commonalities there were. After discussion, we agreed collectively on the top five values for our agency. We have used this values exercise several times, and it is very powerful with both large and small groups.

With this process, everybody buys into the shared values. As you seek to make gender diversity a priority in your organization, it is essential to select values that everyone believes in. This is much more effective than the leader saying, "Okay, everybody, here are our values. You'd better abide by them."

Then, when the organization faces conflicts or challenges, those five values become your road map. You will make decisions based on your top values. When making a major decision, you can ask, "Are we acting in accordance with the values we agreed on?"

If a mouse in the corner were observing your organization and looked at that list of your top five values, we hope the mouse would be able to say, "I see those top values in action"— not "Oh, that's just a charade. Those people don't really live by those values." There is nothing worse than an agent hearing the leader say, "We value individuality," for example, while in private, advisors are rolling eyes and thinking or saying, "Oh, that's a joke!" That is worse than never having said what your value was.

Several websites list values that you and your group can choose from, as well as instructions for completing this values exercise. The MindTools site lists 144 values.[20] A Carnegie Mellon web page lists 124 values.[21]

I (Linda) used to do a lot of team conflict facilitation, and this is exactly the process we used to get team members on the same page. It is an effective problem solver for teams of agents too. People don't always agree on how to approach situations; that is the world we live in. Whether you are a man or a woman, the key to being a good facilitator in this type of process is to ask questions and to let everybody share and be part of the process.

Once you have defined your organization's shared values, communicate them wherever you can—on your website, on posters throughout the building, on meeting agendas, in newsletters, and in team reports. If we were to walk up to anyone in your organization, every single person should readily be able to tell us what the values are.

Elements of a Culture That Women Would Find Inviting

Aaron Skonnard is the CEO of Pluralsight, a technology company. Like our industry, the high-tech industry is male-dominated; only 26 percent of the workforce is female.

Skonnard has a no-nonsense approach for hiring more women. He says, "If you're in a company or industry that needs more women, you need to stop asking why and start helping to create the kind of cultural changes that will entice more women to join your organization."

When people are free to take care of their priorities outside the office, it creates a culture of engagement in-house.

His suggestions include holding recruiters accountable for building a gender-diverse staff, offering mentorship and sponsorship opportunities to attract and support women, and building policies and benefits packages that allow parents of either gender to succeed both at work and home.

For example, Pluralsight is among a growing number of companies that provide all employees with unlimited vacation time. Skonnard says, "We've found that not only does our open-

20 "What Are Your Values?" MindTools website, https://www.mindtools.com/pages/article/newTED_85.htm.
21 "Values Exercise," Carnegie Mellon University, http://www.cmu.edu/career////my-career-path/my-self/values-exercise2.pdf.

ended PTO policy make people of both genders more productive at work, but it makes them happier in the office too. When people are free to take care of their priorities outside the office, it creates a culture of engagement in-house."[22] Obviously, flexibility is one aspect of our industry that is very helpful to all agents when it is well managed. As leaders, it is our responsibility to help all agents manage this flexibility well.

When recruiting women, they want to know what types of support you will offer them once they're on board. Share this information with them during the interview process. Susan L. Combs makes this suggestion:

> Tell women how you plan to make them successful. A lot of managers we work with talk about Women in Insurance & Financial Services (WIFS) and its formal mentorship program. They will tell female candidates, "We are going to get you into the next WIFS mentorship class because we know that is going to help you be paired up with a woman who has been successful in the industry. We are going to send you to a conference and help you get designations. We are going to invest in you and help develop you so that you can advance in this career." You are asking candidates to develop your company for a third of their waking hours. So talking to women about how they fit into your culture and how they can be successful in the business is very important when you are recruiting women.

Tell women how you plan to make them successful.

The following characteristics of an organizational culture are likely to appeal to women. We encourage you to add to this list and use it to guide you and your management team as you build gender diversity into your culture—or as you build your culture around gender diversity.

In general, most women are likely to appreciate a culture that is:

1. Supportive, not competitive. Do advisors encourage and congratulate each other? Is there room at the top for many instead of only one?

2. Team-oriented, not composed of individuals competing against one another

3. Accepting, not critiquing

4. Conducive to building confidence

5. Open, honest, and authentic, with open lines of communication

6. Caring toward individuals and their families

7. Built on high standards that help each person maximize his or her potential

8. Empowering. Help advisors become great "bosses" to themselves. I (Linda) used to say, "I am your leader; you're your own boss...unless you go to jail for securities fraud, and then I have to go with you."

9. Focused on creativity and a "can-do" attitude to overcome challenges

---

22 Aaron Skonnard, "Creating a Culture That Women Want to Join," from the October 2015 issue of *Inc.* magazine and the *Inc.* website, http://www.inc.com/aaron-skonnard/creating-a-culture-that-women-want-to-join.html.

10. Sensitive to the way all actions and words sound to everyone in the organization
11. Flexible, not rigid, with regard to scheduling, the business plan, vertical markets, etc., with a focus on results rather than time spent
12. Community-service-oriented
13. Constantly connected to a passionate desire to help clients through appropriate risk and investment product sales

> *A team-based culture will appeal to many women.*

A team-based culture will appeal to many women. (A team can be you and one advisor or manager; you don't have to have a lot of people in your organization to have a team-oriented culture.) If the culture in your organization is that everybody stands on their own and they all compete with each other, it will be difficult to have a collaborative, supportive culture that supports everyone, both men and women, especially when they have personal challenges.

Most people coming out of college today are used to working on team-based projects. In the past ten years, when interviewing candidates, we (Linda and team) have asked, "On what kind of projects have you collaborated with a team?" It is quite common among younger candidates. Team selling is one way we can make sure reps are pulling their weight on a team instead of trying to be the solo practitioner with the big ego.

Jocelyn Wright of The American College believes in the value of a team environment. She says this:

> For the men who have been successful in the business, especially the older producers, it was really a team of just one. They had to grow their businesses by themselves to become successful. But now there is more of an effort to work in teams because that gives people a sense of being a part of the community. You don't feel like you are one man or woman on an island, trying to figure everything out for yourself. You have someone you can count on. If you are not strong in a particular area, the other person on your team has your back in that regard.
>
> As a manager, you have to see yourself almost as a coach for a world-class sports team. You have to be able to fit all of your players together so that you have great individuals, who are even stronger as a team. Managers might need additional training to be able to see that and to be able to form really powerful teams.

I (Daralee) say frequently, "Together is better. Solo is too slow." Collaboration is optimal and culturally appealing to the natural tendencies of most women, as well as Millennials.

Rethink the African Spear and Bear Statues

Susan L. Combs, president of Combs & Company in New York City, tells this story about a male manager whose office was unapologetically masculine. She offered him some honest feedback about it. Here is her story:

I had a manager who wanted me to kind of give him the "Women 101," and I was waiting in his conference room. It was full of leather furniture, bull and bear statues, and black and white New York City photographs. The last two kickers were that there was a four-foot family crest painted on the wall, and an African spear was leaning up against the wall. It all felt very masculine. He walked in and said, "Susan, what do you think about our conference room?"

I looked at him and said, "Could you get any more testosterone in here?"

He asked, "What?"

"Yeah, you have a freaking African spear leaning up against the wall. You want to bring women in here? They are not going to feel comfortable in here."

We kind of laughed about it, and then he said to me, "We just came out with a commercial, and I would like your opinion."

I said, "Do you really want my opinion, or do you want me to tell you it's great? If you want my opinion, you should sit across from me while we watch it because my face shows everything."

So he sat across from me, and I watched the commercial. After it was done, he said, "Oh, man, is it that bad?"

I replied, "Well, let's look at the positive. You did a great job with diversity. You have all different races, all different ages, but you have one female in the entire commercial. You have her as the prospect, you have her as the receptionist, and you have her as the producer. You didn't even change her hair, her makeup, or her clothes. If a guy watches that commercial, he is not going to see anything, but if you show this to other women, we are all going to see that, sticking out like a sore thumb."

When you are talking to women, I don't think you have to change how you talk, walk, and do everything, but you just have to soften it. I tell the men in my offices all the time, "Talk to your women producers, talk to your clients, and ask them how they feel in the room." I think that a male-dominated culture and environment isn't going to be comfortable for women, and the men are not going to be comfortable bringing in female clients, either.

The environment also needs to be flexible. I have an all-female firm, and we have an open vacation policy; we are very flexible with our moms. They are able to take their kids to school every morning and be home in time to pick them up from school in the afternoons. Granted, they are working some other hours, like after the kids are asleep, but giving them that flexibility makes them so much more productive, and it makes them almost have a greater appreciation for how I run things because they know that I am okay with them going to their kid's school program in the morning And I am okay with them being a Halloween mom or the classroom mom, and I am okay with them taking some extra days when their kids are off school for Christmas vacation. I think women probably work more hours than a lot of the guys do just because they are so grateful that

> *I have an all-female firm, and we have an open vacation policy; we are very flexible with our moms.*

they can have a flexible work environment. They all told me that all their friends are jealous that they are able to work in a flexible environment like that.

Reevaluate Your Rewards and Incentives

Another aspect of culture that needs to be inclusive is the way we recognize and reward achievement and performance. We want to make sure the incentives and rewards we provide are appropriate for women. The same goes for promotions and events—they shouldn't all be golfing tournaments, baseball games, and fishing expeditions. Consider offering spa services, sightseeing trips, musical events, or theater tickets too. And look at the scheduling. If you plan an event for Saturday morning, for example, then parents of young children who have soccer games to attend might not be able to make it.

It is men's responsibility to notice if an event is geared toward men, but it's women's responsibility to speak up and say that those incentives or events do not appeal to them.

We also want to make sure that our rewards and incentives appeal to all age groups. Something that appeals to a Baby Boomer or Gen X'er might not interest a Millennial. Make your decisions based on the group you are rewarding or incentivizing. What will really motivate them? If you're not sure, ask them!

One solution is to pass around a catalog that contains different types of gifts at different award levels, and let each award recipient pick out a gift in the appropriate price range. We (Linda and team) did this at the agency level. We also allowed advisors to write in ideas for rewards if they didn't see anything they liked. And several of our advisors started taking some of their rewards as charitable donations to their favorite charities. This allows advisors to choose what they like, and then managers don't have to guess what might appeal to them.

Consider conducting an informal focus group composed of women you know.

Ask Women What They Think

If you are not sure which elements of your culture are inviting to women and which could use improvement, consider conducting an informal focus group composed of women you know. You could ask female family members, administrative staff members, community leaders, women business owners, bankers, teachers, real estate agents, and even clients to give you an honest assessment and offer suggestions. Women's opinions matter.

For every single decision you make, every action you take, and every word you speak, ask yourself, "How does this look, feel, or sound to the women in the organization, or to prospective female agents or clients?"

I (Linda) was blessed that before I arrived at my agency in the early 1980s, Louise Evenson, a woman manager, was a frontline leader of the organization. She would say, "How does that sound to others? You can't say that. How does this look? How does this feel?" So by the time I went into leadership, I didn't have to do much of that. The male manager, Karsten Lundring, had become the "spokesperson" for gender diversity. It is great when a leader in the organization—either a man or a woman—acts and thinks on women's behalf so that they don't have to speak up and say, "This feels weird to me as a woman. I don't like it." If you are a male leader, take the initiative and spare the women in your organization from the necessity of pointing out cultural aspects that make them uncomfortable.

So when can you start establishing a culture that is conducive to achieving gender diversity? The next time a word comes out of your mouth. You can start at 8:00 a.m. tomorrow because "inch by inch is a cinch." Give yourself permission to take the first step. If it works, continue forward. If not, then regroup. You don't have to have a big, complex plan. Just do your best to be sensitive to women's needs, and try to do better each day.

Questions to Ask Yourself

1. What are your organization's values? If you have not defined them yet, consider doing the values exercise we mentioned with your management team or the entire organization to come up with shared values everyone agrees on.

2. Do you know which elements about your culture would be inviting to women and which might not? Write a list of both.

3. If you do not know how you could make your culture more inviting to women advisors and clients, which women in your circle of influence could you ask for honest feedback?

4. How flexible is your culture in general? And during your advisors' and managers' life challenges?

CHAPTER 5

What Did I Say?
What Did You Hear?

"Gender intelligence is an active consciousness that views gender differences as strengths, not weaknesses."

—From *Work with Me*
By Barbara Annis and John Gray

A husband and wife are on a long-distance road trip, and he is driving. The woman, feeling hungry, sees that they are coming up to an exit where they can get off the highway and go to a restaurant. She asks her husband, "Are you hungry?"

The man replies, "No" and keeps on driving.

The woman sits there fuming because she is starving and wanted to take that exit, but she doesn't say anything.

In this scenario, the man hears the woman ask a question—"Are you hungry?"—and he answers no because he's not hungry.

Now, if that woman were to ask another woman the same question, the second woman is likely to reply, "Not really. But how about you? Are you hungry?"

The first woman might say, "Yes, I am."

So then the woman who was driving would say, "Okay, let's take this next exit and get something to eat."

The reason the conversation between two women goes in a totally different direction than the one between a man and a woman is because women's tendency is to ask questions rather than to assert their own feelings first.

So, in that example, what the woman asked was, "Are you hungry?" But her intended meaning was, "I'm hungry and would like to take the next exit to stop and get something to eat." But what the man heard was, "Are you personally hungry right now?"

This is an example of a typical communication mishap between men and women. It's one of many described by Bruce Christopher, a psychologist, humorist, and interpersonal communication expert.[23]

In general, Bruce says men think compartmentally or in "boxes," and women are more "global" in their thought

Men think compartmentally or in "boxes," and women are more "global" in their thought processes and speech.

---

23 Bruce Christopher speaks at seminars, conventions, conferences, and other meetings more than 150 times a year, and he is one of the most sought-after speakers in the Fortune 500. You can learn more about him at http://www.bcseminars.com/.

processes and speech. Men speak in a bottom-line fashion and don't use as many details. Women tend to speak historically and in a narrative format, with the bottom line coming at the end of the conversation. Men get frustrated when women don't get to the bottom line soon, so they interrupt. Men tend to use persuasion, and women tend to negotiate.

In the workplace, Bruce says women are better at getting the sale because they have a high trust factor. They are better at accommodating and adjusting, whereas men tend to push the point and get aggressive. "It doesn't matter what the product is—communication is what matters," he concludes.

Our Differences Enrich Our Work

> It's likely that the male and female advisors will have different perspectives on the client's situation.

Because men and women have different communication and selling styles, forming teams or joint-work situations in which a man and woman work together is a smart strategy. It gives the client two approaches and personalities to work with. Also, it's likely that the male and female advisors will have different perspectives on the client's situation. That provides a more robust experience for the client and enhances the firm or agency's ability to tailor an optimum solution for the client's financial well-being. This is a significant reason why women matter to your organization.

At Thrivent, we (Linda and team) promoted joint work between male and female advisors. It was fascinating how the males and females often came out of a client appointment with different perspectives. It made them better at serving the client because the women were more sensitive to the nuances, and the men were more direct about getting to the bottom line.

In some cases, men tend to be more product-driven, and women can be more solution-driven. Men sometimes suggest a product to a client and then explain why that product is what the client needs. But women will ask the client about his or her situation, consider the details, and then craft a solution that takes all of those details into consideration. That is why many female clients feel more comfortable working with women advisors—because they are comfortable solving problems this way.

I (Daralee) came into this business to help people solve their problems through the vehicle of a comprehensive financial plan. I didn't come into it because I thought everybody needed a particular product solution. That is the way I grew up in this business. You gather all the data, and then you figure out what it is going to take for clients to get from point A to their desired point B. The point is not to go in there and sell them a particular product, in absence of a tailored plan. I think that is a huge strength that women bring. Women are excellent problem solvers and solution/process providers.

Confirming That We Communicated: A Shared Responsibility

In any conversation, the speaker and the listener are equally responsible for ensuring that communication has taken place effectively.

Many times, we don't take the time to confirm what was just discussed. It's a good idea to get in the habit of confirming, when a conversation ends, what should happen next. You might say, "Now, you are going to get me those reports by tomorrow at noon, right?" Or "I want to make sure I understood you correctly. James and Sarah will begin their joint work tomorrow with their visit to Mr. and Mrs. Weiss. Is that right?"

Many times, we don't take the time to confirm what was just discussed.

If I am the speaker and I think you heard something differently than what I intended, it is my responsibility to restate it in such a way that you understand. And if I am the listener and I don't understand what you say or I think I may not understand, then it is my responsibility to ask more questions. It is a mutual responsibility. This process is good communication and should not be confrontational, fault finding, defensive, or accusatory. This process should be routine, standard procedure in our organizations.

If a man states something in an authoritarian manner, many women will not question it. They don't want to get into a confrontation over something that isn't urgent. If a woman makes a statement, other women would feel more comfortable about asking questions to confirm their understanding.

Eight Blind Spots That Interfere with Our Communication

The book *Work with Me: The Eight Blind Spots between Men and Women in Business* reveals the results of more than 100,000 in-depth interviews of men and women executives in more than sixty Fortune 500 companies. The book is written by two experts on communication between the genders: Barbara Annis, a world-renowned expert on Gender Intelligence® and inclusive leadership; and John Gray, PhD, a leading relationship expert in the world and the bestselling relationship author of all time. *USA Today* ranks his book, *Men Are from Mars, Women Are from Venus*, as one of the top ten most influential books over the past twenty-five years.

A recent *Forbes* article summarized the eight blind spots the authors identified, as well as potential solutions for improving communication between men and women in these areas.[24] We have created our own summary of those blind spots and solutions to them.

---

24 Susan Adams, "Eight Blind Spots between the Sexes at Work," April 2, 2013, *Forbes* website, http://www.forbes.com/sites/susanadams/2013/04/26/8-blind-spots-between-the-sexes-at-work/.

The "Blind Spots" of Communication between Men and Women	How Women Can Overcome Them	How Men Can Overcome Them
1. Conflicting communication styles	Understand that men prioritize and sequence their work on results rather than on the effort to get there.	Realize that women care about goals, but they also care about the process of reaching them.
2. Different modes of appreciation	Acknowledge men's accomplishments.	Understand and appreciate women's efforts on the way to achieving a goal.
3. Women's perception that men exclude them	• Recognize that men prefer to assign and prioritize work, make sure they are not duplicating one another's efforts, and ensure that everyone is working as efficiently as possible. • Understand that, to deal with stress, most men need to shut down and reenergize internally, instead of talking out their problems.	• Recognize that women on teams want to share ideas, maintain strong working relationships, and give everyone a chance to speak. • Understand that, to deal with stress, women want to talk about what's bothering them to someone who will empathize and support them.
4. Men's belief that they have to "walk on eggshells" around women	Try to curb your emotions and frame your conversations directly.	Stop walking on eggshells and instead try empathy, supportiveness, and direct communication.
5. Men's annoyance with the fact that women tend to ask a lot of questions	Respect the male tendency to take risks and understand that men's ability to pay attention is limited.	Recognize that women ask questions not just to get answers but to build consensus, show concern for a project or for others, offer feedback, and ask for support. Accept that there is value in the questions women ask. Listen when women ask questions.

The "Blind Spots" of Communication between Men and Women	How Women Can Overcome Them	How Men Can Overcome Them
6. Differences in the way men and women pay attention	• Understand that when a man is under stress, he tends to develop tunnel vision. • If the man seems inattentive, ask him if he can pause from his work and hear her out.	• Understand that women multitask more naturally and find it difficult to believe that men can't. • If you are too busy to talk with your female colleague, apologize and say you need to finish your task and will talk with her later.
7. Different ways of expressing emotion	• Recognize that women tend to express their emotions more freely, including to strangers. • Realize that expressing concern is cathartic for a woman and a path to finding a solution.	• Recognize that men tend to hide their feelings and reveal them only when they're under high stress—and then only to close confidantes. • Realize that even though a man tends to focus on a solution instead of his feelings about how the problem arose, he is just as concerned as you are about what went wrong.
8. Insensitivity to one another	Both genders: Acknowledge these differences, empathize with one another, and come up with ways to cope with their different responses to workplace challenges.	

People Learn Differently

There are forty or so primary learning modalities. We all process information differently and use a combination of modalities to do so. The most prevalent ones are visual, auditory, and kinesthetic. Visual learners (30 to 40 percent of the population) respond best to pictures, graphs, and other visual stimuli. Auditory learners (20 to 30 percent of the population) are more responsive to words and other sounds. Kinesthetic learners (30 to 50 percent of the population) are most engaged by physical activities.[25]

> *The best way to communicate your message effectively is to provide a combination of visual, auditory, and kinesthetic elements.*

Because every audience and group will have a mixture of all three types of learners, the best way to communicate your message effectively is to provide a combination of visual, auditory, and kinesthetic elements—something for everyone. These differences are not dependent on gender. As leaders, we need to understand that everyone learns differently, so we need to be sensitive to the different learning modalities.

Similarly, not everyone communicates the same way. I (Daralee) used to feel that I had to write something down for my brain to easily grab it. But over the years, I've gotten accustomed to typing into my phone and using the cloud. I don't have to touch paper anymore. Some people prefer to communicate only through texting. These differences are not dependent on gender, either. And sometimes they can be related to a particular generation, but that isn't always the case. We can't assume that just because someone is older, she doesn't use a computer or that because someone is younger, he will communicate only via texting. The way people process information varies, regardless of gender or age. Again, we need to be sensitive to the fact that people communicate differently. We should not impose our most comfortable style on everyone else. Make it a habit to ask others what method of communication they prefer.

Gender-Neutral Communication Is a Part of Your Inclusive Culture

Effective communication is one of the foundations of a strong culture. You can have the best intentions of being gender-inclusive and sensitive to both genders, but if the language you use isn't inclusive and sensitive, you are sabotaging your goal—maybe without realizing it. Awareness is the key. If you know that something is happening in your firm or agency that isn't congruent with the vision and mission you have defined, you will know you need to change it.

A lot of times in meetings, we hear managers say things like, "We are going to invite all of the advisors and their wives." That language needs to change because some advisors are females with husbands, and some advisors have significant others and are not married. A more inclusive statement is, "We are going to invite all of the advisors and their partners."

E-mails can be a potential trouble spot. It is not uncommon for a masculine salutation to be used, such as "Gentlemen" when an e-mail has a distribution list that includes women. This definitely is not appropriate in a gender-diverse organization. A gender-neutral greeting should be used instead.

---

25 *Business Communication* (Boston: Harvard Business School Publishing Corporation, 2003), 88.

My (Linda's) co-Managing Partner at Thrivent, Karsten Lundring, was wonderfully in tune with this entire issue. When we would have industry speakers come to our agency, he would take them aside before their presentations. He would say, "We try to use very gender-neutral language here, so please don't refer to the advisors as 'men.' And please don't refer to the spouses as 'wives.' And if you are giving a life insurance example, don't always use a male who is thirty-five; use a professional who is forty-two or something like that."

Some of the speakers would say, "Seriously, that isn't important, is it?"

Karsten, to his credit, always said, "Yes, that is really important."

But still, many speakers would get on stage and say something like, "It's really nice to see all of you guys here." Karsten and our team tried very hard to expunge the word "guys" from our vocabulary. Yet in the English language, it is very hard to talk about a large group in a casual way without using "you guys." That is, unless you are from the South, and then you can say, "All y'all."

Now, if you say, "It's great to be here with all of you guys. Oh, and you gals too," that is just as bad or worse. It makes the women in the room feel like they are afterthoughts. We recommend saying something gender-neutral like "everyone" or "all of the advisors" or "all of the agents." For example, you could say, "It is great to be here with everyone" or "It is great to be here with all of you advisors."

My (Daralee's) husband is a filmmaker. When directing everybody on the set, he uses the word "people"—for example, "People, we're wrapping this set and moving to the kitchen scene." It might seem a little impersonal or distancing, but it is gender-neutral and can be a good word to use.

I (Thomasina) once sat in a meeting in which a new Senior Vice President who was taking over our territory introduced himself. Only a few women were in the room. He immediately told us about his wife, who had a shopping problem—"like most women." All the men had a good laugh with him. I knew exactly what he thought of me! After that, I would jokingly threaten my male peers that I was going to take their wives shopping.

Be Considerate

Some years ago, I (Linda) went on an Alaskan fishing trip with my husband and seven of his male friends and cousins. They had gone two years earlier and had a great time—beautiful scenery, whales jumping—it sounded great. So I said, "Well, the next time you go, I want to go along." I don't even care about fishing, but I wanted to go for the scenery.

We had two people in each small fifteen-foot aluminum open boat, and the idea was to go fishing a little bit offshore. We had radios to communicate with the other boats. The waves were getting pretty high, and as we navigated slowly through these high seas, I looked back at the other boats and noticed that one of them had disappeared. I asked my husband, "Where did they go?"

He replied, "If they need help, they will call on the radio."

But, I thought, what if they had capsized and lost their radios? What if a wave knocked them unconscious? They couldn't call for help. If I had been with another woman in my boat, we would have gone back to make sure the people in that boat were okay because they weren't communicating. When something doesn't seem right, women will go investigate. Men just figure everything is okay until they hear otherwise.

As it turns out, the two men in the missing boat had gone down to a little cove and stopped for a "bathroom break" in the woods ashore.

We all need to be constantly aware of how our actions affect other people.

If women had been in that "missing boat," they probably would have contacted everyone else on the radio in advance and said, "Hey, we're stopping off at this little cove for a few minutes. We won't be on the radio for a little while." They wouldn't want everyone to worry about them.

We all need to be constantly aware of how our actions affect other people.

Women: Assert Yourself!

Many relationship experts describe how men will interrupt one another during a heated conversation, while women will sit there silently waiting to be invited to the conversation and then feel excluded.

This has been our collective experience as women who have risen to leadership positions in a mostly male industry. While the men interrupt one another, we have sat back too many times, thinking that what we had to say was also important, but we did not want to be rude. We had to learn to speak up and interrupt. If we didn't do so, those important points we wanted to make would never be heard.

If we waited until we were asked to speak, it would never happen because that isn't the way it is. So this is our chance to give advice to both the males and females. We want to encourage women to jump into conversations and be more assertive than you normally might be. And we want to encourage men to recognize that this is how women tend to operate. If you're leading a meeting and only the men have provided their input, ask the women for their opinions as well.

Women: Stop Apologizing!

Another interesting communication difference is that women tend to apologize a lot more than men. We apologize when it's not necessary, for a variety of reasons. Doing so can be seen as a sign of weakness, and it undermines our power.

In 2010, two studies conducted by researchers at the University of Waterloo in Ontario and published in the journal *Psychological Science* found that, although men are just as willing as women to apologize, they have a higher threshold for what they feel they need to apologize for. In one of the two studies, men said they would apologize less frequently than women for doing things such as inconveniencing someone they live with or being rude to a friend.[26]

Why do we feel compelled to apologize for everything? Various experts theorize that we do it to because we want to seem likable, accessible, and less threatening if we are in positions of authority. Women, let's stop apologizing unnecessarily and start speaking more

---

26 Kelly Wallace, "Sorry to Ask, But...Do Women Apologize More than Men?" June 26, 2014, CNN website, http://www.cnn.com/2014/06/26/living/women-apologize-sorry-pantene-parents/.

directly about what we think and want. This one step alone can help us all communicate better.

Just being aware of the ways in which men and women communicate differently can help us close the gender communication gap—at work, at home, and everywhere else. Wouldn't life be easier if we communicated more effectively with our colleagues, our partners, the barista at Starbucks, and our real estate agent?

Examples of More Inclusive Language

We'll close this chapter with some examples of how the simplest communication can go awry—and how to choose more inclusive language that will make the women feel just as welcome as the men.

When You Say This ...	A Woman Might Hear or Perceive This	Try This Instead
"Hello, guys...."	"I am not included in this group."	"Hello, everyone" or "Hello, advisors."
"We want you all to bring your wives."	"Only married men are included, and single people are excluded."	"Your significant others are, of course, invited."
"Who remembers Pittsburgh Steeler Franco Harris's 'immaculate reception' in the AFC divisional playoff game in December 1972?"	"Only sports fans are included."	Avoid using sports examples to make a point. Find a recent YouTube example that is non-sports-related.
"Calm down. You're overreacting!"	"That is judgmental language and shows a lack of desire to understand."	"Help me understand what is going on."
"You don't want this promotion. You won't have time for your kids."	"This represents an unequal opportunity for women and discrimination against parents."	"Would you like to be considered for this promotion?" or "This promotion brings more responsibilities. What strategies are you planning to handle them?"
"You sure are pretty."	That is an unprofessional comment in the workplace.	Avoid comments about appearance.

When You Say This ...	A Woman Might Hear or Perceive This	Try This Instead
"Could you get to the point already?"	He does not have time for me and is being dismissive.	Say nothing. Make the time to listen and confirm understanding. Or say, "After your analysis, what is your conclusion?"

Questions to Ask Yourself

1. Think about conversations you've witnessed in meetings, at lunches, and in the hallway at your firm or agency. What are some words or phrases that might make women think they are being excluded? What will you do to communicate to your entire organization that this language is no longer considered acceptable?

2. Think about some of the times you have had difficulty communicating with someone of the opposite sex. What do you think was the reason for the miscommunication? What could you or the other person have done differently to make it a smoother process?

3. Are you mostly a visual, auditory, or kinesthetic learner? Do you tend to communicate with other people based on your own learning modality? If so, how will you change your communication methods to make your message clearer to everyone in your firm or agency?

4. If you are a woman, do you apologize too often and shrink back in meetings, waiting for someone to ask your opinion? If so, now that you are aware of it, what steps will you take to be more assertive?

5. If you are a man, what steps will you take when you observe a woman in a meeting who appears to be uncomfortable contributing?

CHAPTER 6

Recruiting Successful Women

"The successful growing firms are focused on recruiting women and multicultural producers to better serve the markets in their communities. A performance-based culture needs to be a mixed culture, with mutual respect for people's differences and appreciation for the value they bring that may be different than others."

—Pamela Blalock, National Life Group[27]

As you recruit women, it's important to look at all aspects of your culture and environment and ensure that they are conducive to attracting women. This includes making sure your job postings, job descriptions, and other recruitment materials are gender-neutral and inclusive. You'll also want to make sure your office is inviting to both women and men. If you have magazines in your lobby, offer titles that will appeal to both genders—not just *Golf Digest* and *Car and Driver*.

It is human nature for us to hire people like ourselves. Therefore, men need a specific strategy to recruit women. If you are a man recruiting female candidates, it is important to be open-minded and to expect that there will be cultural differences between you as the recruiter and your potential candidates.

Once you have a few women advisors on board, it will be much easier to recruit additional women. Your female advisors will be valuable sources for referrals. Also, when female candidates ask how many women are already on board in your organization (or look at your website), they will be more likely to consider your firm or agency as an option if they see that you have other female advisors.

> *Once you have a few women advisors on board, it will be much easier to recruit additional women.*

Here are some practical tips for finding and attracting high-quality female candidates.

Go Where the Women Are

The biggest challenge about recruiting women, particularly for many male managers, is figuring out where to find potential recruits.

Finding professional successful women may mean that you have to join or sponsor a female organization. Get to know the people in that organization, and contribute however you can. Let people know the type of candidate you are looking for.

---

27 "Recruiting Women to the Advisor Career," GAMA Foundation, p. 22.

Also, you might have to ask for help from females in your environment, such as administrative staff or the professional spouses of your male advisors. Ask them for their input. You need women who can help you identify quality female candidates, or at least put you in the right environment so that you have access to high-quality, high-performing female candidates.

You also can find great candidates by getting involved in community-service initiatives. The type of people you are looking for are comfortable serving others and working on committees. Women who serve on nonprofit boards of directors tend to care about their communities; this is a great place to recruit.

Susan L. Combs has these suggestions for where to find high-quality female candidates:

> I have found some good people from women's MBA groups. For example, there is a business school here, and a lot of later-in-life people are getting their MBAs. I think that is a good place to look for people. I also think career changers are always good candidates—people who have been teachers for twenty years, and they have a great pension. They are not done educating, and they want to look at educating people in a different aspect. And we shouldn't discount moms. Half of my workforce is composed of moms who have little kids. I give them flexibility so that they can be successful and still be present mothers. They can make money in this industry.

I have found some good people from women's MBA groups.

Diane Dixon, owner of 3F Coaching, suggests asking community leaders for referrals to women candidates:

> Once you know your "why" for recruiting women and your game plan is together, make a list of community leaders, especially women community leaders, And invite them to lunch individually. Sit down with them and say very candidly, "I work in an industry that offers an amazing career. We think it is an ideal career for women, but quite frankly, we haven't done a very good job of promoting it to women. We want to do a better job of promoting it and making it a better place for them, and we would like your help in identifying women who might be good candidates for this career." Women don't want you pandering for women referrals, but if you are serious, know your why, know why this career is ideal for women, and know what you are looking for in a strong candidate, they can help guide you.
>
> You can even invite a dozen of the women leaders in your community to come in and talk about the career and your firm or agency. Then you can engage them to be advocates who help you promote the career.
>
> If I were a Managing Partner, I might consider having someone from outside the organization come in and assess how well our team is doing at hiring women or minorities or even serving consumers. Some people don't know how bad their culture is. Sometimes we are just oblivious to some of the very obvious things. Why

not have women come in and serve as "mystery shoppers"? They could interview and go through the entire recruiting process. Then get a report from them on what was attractive to them and what wasn't. I think that could be invaluable.

Educate Women about the Great Aspects of a Career as an Advisor

As leaders in this industry, we have a unique opportunity to increase awareness among women—preferably young women—about the benefits of this career.

I (Daralee) am attracting more women to this career by meeting with deans and career counselors at local colleges and universities. By being an accessible community resource, we can help raise awareness about this career. Students are invited to participate in informational classes about what we do, or to be interns. By being visible on campuses, we can reach more women. Men tend to be attracted to this career; they are the ones who more frequently bubble to the surface when we are recruiting. It requires a deliberate effort to make sure that women know about the viability of this career. We share that this career is great for women because:

> *By being an accessible community resource, we can help raise awareness about this career.*

1. Your primary focus is to help people. (You can do well by doing good.)
2. There is no limit to your income potential.
3. There is no "glass ceiling."
4. Your raise is not determined by subjective metrics.
5. You can impact multiple generations through your work.
6. You can enjoy a flexible schedule that allows you to blend your work and professional responsibilities with your other personal interests and responsibilities.

The interview process is obviously a major part of educating candidates about the career. Susan L. Combs offers this insight about interviewing Millennials:

> During the interview process, Millennials need to ask questions. If they are not asking questions, then you don't have them. Sometimes you have to feed them those questions. I recommend having a list of five questions ready. When you are interviewing them, you could say, "Do you have any questions about what this career looks like? I know that John just started here last year, and these are some of the questions he had." Then the candidate won't feel like an idiot for not coming up with it on her own; she can say, "Yes, I am curious about that."
>
> Millennials value time. One of my producers, a Millennial, is not interested in hearing that she can be making six figures on a consistent basis in three years. She wants to hear that she can start working from home on Fridays and Mondays in three years if she sets this up right. Recently, I told her that depending on the

schedule, and if she has her home office set up, she can start working from home on Fridays if she wants to. She loved that; she was ecstatic.

Let Millennials know that you offer flexibility and fun, and let them know what the prize is. A lot of Millennials want instant gratification, but then they go back and go through things step by step. When you are taking Millennials through the training process, you have to start with the bottom line and say, "This is what the result is going to be." And then you work your way backward to step one.

> *Let Millennials know that you offer flexibility and fun, and let them know what the prize is.*

Demonstrate How You Support Women

Stacy Nystrom, a partner and recruiter with Thrivent Financial, says it is important to show female candidates how you support the women who work in your organization:

> Early on, when you are recruiting women, I think it is important to connect female candidates with other women to show them that there are other women who are successful in the business. When you host a women's event and bring in all your women advisors, invite your female recruits as well. Bring in people who are in the interview process and those who are in licensing. Help them feel that there is a network or a community they can latch onto.

Recognize Women's Potential Fears

One detriment to recruiting women into this industry is the potential risk factor. Most women worry if they will be successful and wonder if they can make a living on a commission-based income. Some men are risk-adverse too, but many women fear spending their time in a career where they won't be able to support their families and still do all the things they need to do at home. To help a female candidate deal with this fear, have her talk to successful female advisors to learn how they handle the variable income stream and to hear about the joy and pride of receiving high income based on personal achievements.

When I (Daralee) was twenty-seven, I had a deep drive to be of service and to help people. I also knew that if I was going to have an uncertain income, I had to have the self-confidence to know that if the mission was right, then everything would work out. My goal was to help people with their financial future. So I walked away from a teaching salary, and I had never been on commission. I had a new baby, was getting a divorce, and was going to be on my own. I knew that I had to focus forward for the right cause and find a career with unlimited upside that provided complete flexibility so that I could be both a parent and a professional.

Once I learned more about the career, it appealed to me, and I took the risk. This career has provided a wonderfully rich life for my children and family, one that they would have never had if I had not made the change. We need to let women know that it can be lucrative and fulfilling for them.

What I (Daralee) always discuss with candidates in interviews is that they are going to be able to tailor their career around themselves. Just like we tailor our clients' financial plans to them, advisors can tailor the career. Advisors start with understanding where they are now, where they want to go, and by when. What are their hopes and dreams? What is important to them about money, both professionally and personally? Every day has value and impact; this is a wonderful way to earn a living. I can't imagine any other way.

I (Linda) said to a candidate in the interview process, "No matter how many interviews and tests we give you, the person who knows you best is you. My job in this process is to help you really know and feel what this career entails, both the benefits and the challenges. Then you can be honest with yourself and make an informed decision."

See more ideas for how to help candidates learn about this career in Chapter 7.

Recruit to Your Culture

When recruiting both men and women, our goal is to find candidates who fit our culture. If they are a good culture fit, they will be more likely to stay with the firm or agency and to excel in the position.

As we mentioned in Chapter 4, once you have defined your culture, it's important to make the elements of your culture a prominent part of your everyday communications.

That includes your recruiting materials. To hire candidates who are likely to excel in your culture, include the key elements of your culture in your recruiting ads and job descriptions. This will immediately screen out candidates who do not resonate with your culture.

Susan L. Combs offers this tip for discovering women's passions, which can be a key to knowing whether or not they might be a good fit for your culture:

> When I talk to managers who are looking to bring women in, I tell them that in this day and age, you can't ask if a woman is married or if she has kids or things like that, but you can look at the bottom of a résumé and usually see her volunteer work and board work. So I always tell managers, whether they are male or female, to get women to start talking about those types of things because if they are passionate about different causes, they can definitely be passionate about this industry. I think it is a wonderful industry for women.

Ask Others to Refer Candidates to You

When asking a center of influence for referrals to qualified candidates, be specific about the type of candidate you're looking for. You could say, "We are trying to grow our organization and are particularly looking for talented, professional women to join our firm."

That will get your warm-source referrals thinking about the women they know who fill that description, rather than just thinking about professional men they know. As leaders, we need to "train" our sources to think of women candidates so they can move beyond the stereotypes.

Professional coach Diane Dixon shares this advice for asking for female referrals:

When asking a center of influence for referrals to qualified candidates, be specific about the type of candidate you're looking for.

We receive advisor referrals because the advisors in our office refer us to people they have been working with. If you ask a man, "Who is the most successful person you know?" he will probably think of a lot of the guys he knows because he is a man. So typically, if you have a white guy calling on white people, you get white-guy referrals. This is not science. We used to tell our people that when they were asking for referrals, we wanted them to ask questions that would cause people to think of successful women. Here are some questions to ask:

- "Who is the most successful saleswoman you know?"
- "Who is the most successful entrepreneurial woman you know?"
- "Who is the most standout female who has recently graduated from college that you know?"
- "Do you know any women in pharmaceutical sales?"
- "What woman do you know who has been at home and is now ready to re-enter the workforce and is looking for a career?"

Ask your own advisors for referrals too. Ask about females they know who are accountants, bankers, real estate agents, nurses, teachers, or stay-at-home moms who are ready to re-enter the work force.

Consider working with or establishing a "career re-entry program."

If you are worried about recruiting a woman who has been out of the workforce for a few years, consider working with or establishing a "career re-entry program." These programs provide support to people, such as stay-at-home moms, who have been out of the work force for a while and want to return. An example of one such firm is iRelaunch (https://www.irelaunch.com/), which was founded by Carol Fishman Cohen.

Goldman Sachs is an example of one company that is using this approach. The company launched its "returnship" program in 2008 and received more than three hundred applications in the first year. The program lasts for ten weeks. During that time, participants are paid to re-immerse themselves in different departments and projects at Goldman Sachs. The company hires nearly half of the participants as full-time employees following the program.[28]

Create a Work Environment That Motivates People

When people are looking for a career, they have certain job elements in mind that motivate them personally. To attract the best candidates, it helps to know what motivates people. A lot of people in our industry believe that money is the biggest motivator. But many research studies show that money isn't even among the top five motivators.

Psychologist Daniel Pink says money is a "carrot and stick" approach that is not an effective motivator. Instead, he says the secret to high performance and satisfaction—at

---

28 Charles Coy, "How Career Re-Entry Programs Are Tackling the Gender Gap One Hire at a Time," May 29, 2015, Cornerstone on Demand website, http://www.cornerstoneondemand.com/blog/how-career-re-entry-programs-are-tackling-gender-gap-one-hire-time#.Vgw575fRXIU.

work, at school, and at home—is the deeply human need to direct our own lives, to learn and create new things, and to do better by ourselves and our world. In his best-selling book *Drive: The Surprising Truth about What Motivates Us*, he writes that people are driven by autonomy, mastery, and purpose.[29]

In a 2014 study about key workplace trends, money ranked seventh as a motivator in a survey of more than 200,000 employees in more than 500 organizations. One of the questions was "What motivates you to excel and go the extra mile at your organization?" Employees could choose from ten answers. Money and benefits ranked seventh.

The survey did not distinguish between men's and women's responses. Here are the top ten motivators for employees at all levels of these many organizations:

1. Camaraderie, peer motivation (20 percent)

2. Intrinsic desire to do a good job (17 percent)

3. Feeling encouraged and recognized (13 percent)

4. Having a real impact (10 percent)

5. Growing professionally (8 percent)

6. Meeting client/customer needs (8 percent)

7. Money and benefits (7 percent)

8. Positive supervisor/senior management (4 percent)

9. Belief in the company/product (4 percent)

10. Other (9 percent)[30]

It is clear that a majority of these factors are present in this career and would be attractive to women. Making these characteristics a reality in your firm or agency will help attract high-quality candidates of either gender.

Jocelyn Wright, a professor at The American College, agrees that money is not the primary motivator for women. She says this:

> The old-school way of attracting people is to talk about how much money you can make. But too often, we don't tell candidates all that is required to make that amount of money. And we don't tell them it is not about the money. Women I talk to in this business did not get into this business for money. For most of the women I talk to, their purpose in getting into the business was to make a difference and to do good. That tendency women have to serve is really satisfied, to a great degree, in this business.

Women I talk to in this business did not get into this business for money.

29 Daniel H. Pink, *Drive: The Surprising Truth about What Motivates Us*, Kindle edition (New York: Riverhead Books/The Penguin Group, 2011).

30 "The Seven Key Trends Impacting Today's Workplace," TinyTrends website, https://www.tinypulse.com/2014-employee-engagement-organizational-culture-report.

Try These Recruiting Strategies

The GAMA Foundation study we referred to earlier offers these tips to employ when recruiting women:

1. **Contact women more often.** Plan on having twice as much contact with a female candidate as you do with a male candidate. You may need to contact a female recruit once or twice a week but a male recruit only every two weeks or so.

2. **Be courteous.** Take care not to interrupt when she is talking, and be sure to maintain eye contact. These courtesies may require exercising some patience, but they will make women feel included and valued.

3. **Emphasize the right priorities.** Women tend to prioritize different aspects of the career compared with men, so develop language that best presents the industry and its opportunities for women. In particular, emphasize the ability to help others, flexibility and work/life balance, equal treatment, and an equal opportunity to make money.

4. **Present the level playing field.** Discuss how an advisor's value is based on his or her performance, not gender.

5. **Provide details.** Because women value details, provide specific information on the training and education you provide. Address any concerns the woman may have about needing a specific background or education in finance.

6. **Explain her fit with the industry.** Review how her experience and skills make her a good fit for the occupation. Using real-life examples, outline how the candidate can benefit personally, professionally, and financially.

7. **Be clear about the challenges.** Discuss both the positive and the negative aspects of the industry. Although the industry has many pluses, transitioning into it can be accompanied by setbacks and disappointments. Providing detail, breadth, and depth creates a high degree of trust with recruits.[31]

Simply by focusing on recruiting women, you probably will notice opportunities that you overlooked before.

Simply by focusing on recruiting women, you probably will notice opportunities that you overlooked before. You just need to know what you're looking for, spread the word to those around you, and be open to the ways in which you might need to revise your approach to include women.

---

31 "Recruiting Women to the Advisor Career," GAMA Foundation, p. 9.

Questions to Ask Yourself

1. How can you revise your current vision statement to include gender diversity prominently?

2. Look at your recruiting materials (ads, brochures, web pages). Are they gender-neutral? Do the photos show both men and women, or men only? Are your stories and examples about men and women, or just men?

3. What are some professional and philanthropic organizations in your community that you can join or sponsor to get to know professional women who might be interested in the advisor career?

4. How will you describe your ideal female candidate to your centers of influence? Write it down, and be specific so that you can receive the best possible referrals who will fit with your culture.

5. What types of changes, if any, do you need to make to your physical environment to make it more attractive to women?

6. What types of changes, if any, can you make to ensure that your organization offers the types of motivation to allow both men and women to succeed?

CHAPTER 7

Selecting Successful Women

"Tell me and I'll forget, show me and I might remember, involve me and I will understand."

—Benjamin Franklin

We can't look at a person and instantly tell if he or she has great potential and might fit our culture well. So we have to ask the right questions.

When you ask a question in a candidate interview, know its purpose, and know the type of answer you hope to receive. Also, ask open-ended questions that require candidates to explain their answers. A closed-ended question is one that can be answered with a "yes" or "no." You want to avoid those. For example, you will learn more by asking, "To what extent do you value integrity, and what is an example?" than you will by asking, "Do you have integrity?" Or say, "Tell me about a time when you had to take action based on your integrity."

One of the reasons recruiting women into our industry is a challenge is that the interview questions and selection criteria are often slanted toward men.

We realize that, in many cases, the home office provides interview questions for managers to use in interviews. If some of those questions are geared toward males, just tweak the questions to take out some language or nuances that are male-oriented. Then let your home office know that some of the questions are not gender-neutral. That will give your company a chance to take a step forward in helping our industry become more inclusive of women.

I (Linda) recall that years ago, an interview question in some firms and agencies was "How do you like your steak?" The candidate might answer, "I like my steak well done." So the manager's question to the applicant was, "What would you do if the waiter brought you a rare steak?" The idea was to see if the candidate had enough gumption to talk to the server about the steak being cooked incorrectly.

That question applies only to people who like steak—and it seems that more men than women are steak eaters. Also, it isn't relevant to anybody who is a vegetarian. Other interview questions and examples focused on sports, so they were male-oriented. Of course, some women play sports too, but the idea is to choose gender-neutral, or inclusive, interview questions and examples.

Screen for Specific Traits

Knowing your own culture and what it takes to succeed in this career, identify specific characteristics you want your new advisors to have. Here are some suggestions.

1. A Pattern of Success—And Overcoming Failure

We want to look for patterns of success in a candidate's life. We are looking for people who understand what it is like to be successful, have been successful, and have been in a service-oriented role in some way. We are looking for that "servant leadership" mentality. We want to hire people who have been in charge of their own schedule in the past and have shown success in that type of situation. Select for success without being slanted toward males.

> *A pattern of success might look different for a woman than for a man.*

A pattern of success might look different for a woman than for a man. For either gender, being the captain of a sports team obviously shows leadership. But you don't have to be an Olympic athlete to demonstrate a desire to win. There are many other indications of a candidate's leadership ability. In addition to sports, ask your candidates about the following activities. Think outside your own realm of experience:

- Participation and leadership in college clubs and groups
- Leadership in volunteer community-service initiatives
- Excellence in playing a musical instrument
- Pursuing artistic achievement such as painting, making pottery, scrapbooking, or needlepoint
- Leading or organizing a book club
- Excelling at sewing or quilt making
- Riding horses competitively
- Raising livestock and showing animals at the state fair
- Exceptional life experiences (e.g., mountain climbing, kayaking, traveling, sailing)

Also, ask candidates if they faced any challenges in pursuing these activities. If so, how did they overcome them? What kept them from quitting? How long did they pursue these activities? Did their skills increase—for example, did they rise to first chair in the violin section? Did they take on a leadership role—for example, did they host meetings and recruit for members of their clubs?

Often overlooked is a candidate's experience of failing at an endeavor and how they responded to that failure. I (Linda) had an excellent young woman advisor who quit in her second year because she felt she was a "failure." She had always been at the top of anything she tried, including academic honors, marathon running, and awards for her musical talent. Because she was now the third-highest producer in her group of new hires, she felt she was a failure. In her life experience, she had always been number one. Therefore, a candidate's experience of overcoming failure and pursuing a goal despite having failed at first is just as important to discover in the interview process as a pattern of success.

2. Confidence

In our industry, some managers look for conspicuous competitiveness as a personality trait. That characteristic is not likely to be as common in the female population. People who are competitive are focused on winning, and there is certainly nothing wrong with a desire to win.

But what is the point about being competitive? We want our advisors to be committed to "winning" for our clients' sake, not just their own. We want advisors who have the client's best interest in mind, who offer solutions that are well-founded in facts and research, and who have the confidence to deliver those solutions to give our clients a better quality of life.

We think it's more about confidence, tenacity, assertiveness, and persistence.

We think it's more about confidence, tenacity, assertiveness, and persistence. If an advisor is working with a client and suggests life insurance, but the client doesn't want life insurance, how assertive will that advisor be about explaining to the client the dangers of leaving the risk-management portion of his or her financial plan unresolved? And if the client says he or she will think about getting life insurance, how persistent will that advisor be about reminding the client that time is of the essence, and he or she needs to get life insurance in place now?

Advisors who have confidence, tenacity, assertiveness, and persistence are more likely to do the following well:

- Acquire clients.
- Ask for referrals.
- Network with centers of influence and potential clients.
- Launch effective marketing campaigns.
- Make follow-up phone calls.
- Overcome the rejection associated with acquiring clients.
- Overcome the rejection associated with making proposals to clients. Clients don't always implement all of our recommendations. So we have to be committed, confident, and persistent.
- Ask for the sale.

3. Communication Skills

Because our business requires the ability to connect with people, we need to look for candidates who can communicate well and connect with people. This is all about building relationships. The interview process itself is a good way to gauge a candidate's communication and rapport-building skills.

Does the candidate have a history of public speaking? Is he or she comfortable addressing groups? Does he or she enjoy being a guest speaker? What was the last group the candidate addressed, and what was the topic? These are good questions to ask and excellent indications of good communication skills.

4. Resilience

Everyone faces tough times in life. What separates the successful from those who give up is how we handle those tough times. We need to find out how resilient a candidate is. Because rejection is a big part of what we do, we need advisors who have enough resilience to focus on the positive aspects of a situation and not dwell on the negative aspects.

> *What separates the successful from those who give up is how we handle those tough times.*

To find out how resilient a candidate is, have the candidate describe a difficult time he or she experienced. In the interview, say, "Tell me about a time when you did not succeed at something you cared about. What happened, and how did you handle it? What was the outcome? How did it change you? How well can you bounce back after something doesn't work out? To what extent do you keep coming back time after time?"

As you select from among a highly qualified pool of women candidates, be careful to avoid eliminating someone who may appear to have many challenges. Don't underestimate someone's ability to handle multiple family issues. Don't assume that women candidates who have family responsibilities are inappropriate for this career. I (Linda) once advised a very qualified young woman not to join our organization because she was four months pregnant. I assumed that it would be too difficult to start this career with a newborn. It was my error that I never gave her the opportunity to develop a strategy for this challenge.

While legal reasons prevent us from asking about spouses or children in the interview process, candidates often volunteer this information in the course of answering our open-ended questions. And sometimes we exclude candidates who otherwise have all the traits we seek.

Consider the situation of two successful female managers who started as financial advisors. I (Daralee) might never have been hired if the manager thought that because I was a single mom with a new baby, I would not be able to handle the challenge.

I (Linda) know of another example of starting this career successfully despite family challenges. My Thrivent colleague, Shari Cooper, had a four-year-old, an eighteen-month-old daughter, and was pregnant with twins when she started in this industry. Not only was Sheri a successful advisor; she has developed into a successful Managing Partner and excellent leader. She states that she had a plan to manage the early challenges, which included relying on support from her husband and in-laws.

Use "career sampling" methods as much as legally possible in your organization. This exercise allows candidates to shadow an experienced advisor for several days, learning firsthand the challenges and rewards of this career. Hopefully the experienced advisor will be totally honest with the candidate and share sincere frustrations that might arise. And hopefully the experienced advisor will speak in glowing terms of the supportive culture in your organization that allows people to overcome challenges. The more honestly the realities of this career are communicated to women candidates, the more realistic these women will be about their resilience to start this career.

5. Coachability

It's vital that advisors can be coached. Advisors who are overly confident and think they know everything are not likely to be coachable. When that happens, you have a big problem. Everybody needs coaching—even managers.

Leadership IQ's Global Talent Management Survey studied 5,247 hiring managers from 312 public, private, business, and healthcare organizations over a period of three years. The study found that managers tend to focus their interviews on technical skills because those skills are easy to evaluate. But a lack of technical skills accounts for only 11 percent of new-hire failures.

So what should we focus on? According to the survey, new hires fail most often because of a lack of coachability; in fact, 26 percent of new hires fail due to their inability to accept feedback from those they work with, including managers, colleagues, and customers.

The next three most common reasons new hires fail were a lack of emotional intelligence, a lack of motivation, and a temperament (attitude and personality) not well suited to the job and work environment.

Mark Murphy, CEO of Leadership IQ, asks, "Do technical skills really matter if the employee isn't open to improving, alienates his or her coworkers, lacks emotional intelligence, and has the wrong personality for the job?"[32]

Questions to Ask Yourself

1. Review your selection criteria and interview questions. Are they geared in any way toward men in terms of the language and subject matter? If so, how will you revise them?

2. What traits do you screen for now? Do you need to revise that list in any way to include women? If so, how?

3. What traits do your most successful advisors have in common? Add those characteristics to your selection criteria.

---

32 Mark Murphy, "Why New Hires Fail (Emotional Intelligence vs. Skills)," Leadership IQ website, http://www. leadershipiq.com/blogs/leadershipiq/35354241-why-new-hires-fail-emotional-intelligence-vs-skills.

CHAPTER 8

Supporting Successful Women

"Look what's happened since 1776, most of the time, using half our talent. I mean, just imagine what's going to happen when we go full-blast with 100 percent. It's incumbent on everybody— particularly if you're in a boss's type position, to help people achieve their potential. And women have every bit the potential men do."

—Warren Buffett,
Most successful investor of the twentieth century

We talk about retention a lot in our industry, and for good reason. We spend a lot of time, money, and effort recruiting and selecting ideal candidates. We want them to stay on board for their entire careers. The key to retention is support. We want to make sure we are providing the tools our advisors need to excel in their practices, whether they are male or female, and reach the optimum level of their potential.

Women matter, and their ability to remain in this career for the long term matters. Here are some practical strategies for providing support to help women excel in their careers and achieve work/life balance.

Encourage Women to Ask for What They Need

Many women are so accustomed to worrying about what the other people in their lives need and want that they never learn to articulate what they want and need. Diane Dixon describes how she encourages women to speak up and let people know how to help them— and how to treat them:

> In my coaching business, I encourage women to ask for what they want, whether it is from their clients, their Managing Partner, the home office, or someone on their team. I tell them that they have to teach people how to treat them. It is really up to them to do that. I say that to all my clients, male or female:
> "It is your responsibility to teach people how to treat you." You can't expect people to figure it out. Most people want to know how to please you or how to make you happy. It is helpful to them when we guide them by asking or sharing directly what we want and need. On the other hand, if you are not sure how someone you are working with wants to be treated, then ask them. I'll bet few people have asked them that before.

It is your responsibility to teach people how to treat you.

Recognize That Family Comes First for Most Women

For most women, their children come first, their families come second, and their careers come third.

Arthea (Charlie) Reed and Diane Dixon released their book, *Financial Services: Women at the Top—A WIFS Research Study*, in 2015. The book featured in-depth interviews with twenty-three of the eight hundred women who participated in a recent Women in Insurance & Financial Services (WIFS) survey. Those women represented every level of experience in the insurance and financial services industry and virtually all income levels.

One key fact the survey revealed is that for most women, their children come first, their families come second, and their careers come third. Here is what Charlie has to say about the survey results and the *Women at the Top* book:

When WIFS analyzed those survey data in April 2012, we looked at the results, dividing the responses according to income level. We wanted to get a sense of what the most successful women in the industry who have stayed in the industry over many years are doing or have done that women who leave the industry or are less successful have not. That was the goal of the survey.

The survey provided a lot of really good raw data and information. But we had more questions than answers. We knew, for example, that 94 percent of the women respondents who earned more than $500,000 annually were married or had a life partner. That was a bit of a surprise to many of us because we had thought, and a lot of people think, that women have to be married to their careers to be as successful as these women are.

Likewise, about 90 percent of the women respondents earning more than $500,000 annually have children. Some of these women are now or at times during their careers have been single mothers. The fact that so many more of the most successful women have children than those who are less successful also surprised us and caused us to ask a lot of questions:

- Why were so many more of the highly successful women married or in committed relationships than those who were less successful?

- Were they more likely to be successful if they were married or if they had children? Why?

- How did these incredibly successful women, particularly those with children, juggle life at home and life in the office? How did single mothers build such successful careers?

- How were they able to focus on their children when their jobs were so demanding?

- What kept them in the career while many of the less successful women responding to the survey told us, "It is impossible to have a family and stay in this career"?

We determined that the only way to answer these questions and many more was to conduct in-depth interviews with some of the most successful women in the industry. The interviews with twenty-three of these incredibly successful women, along with the survey results, are the basis for the book *Financial Services: Women at the Top—A WIFS Research Study.*

Many of the women featured in the book had young children when they entered the career or shortly thereafter. Several were single moms; two were young widows. Today, the twenty-three women all have an annual income over $250,000, the vast majority over $500,000. Four have an annual income more than $1 million, and two have earned more than $10 million at least once during their careers.

Most of the twenty-three women featured in the book have a long tenure in this industry—some with more than thirty years of experience—although some have been in the industry less than a decade and still have young children. When we interviewed them, we got more information about how they have done what they have done despite their many commitments.

It is very clear that their children are always number one. Whether their children are preschoolers or are married and have their own children, those children and grandchildren are always number one. These women's families are always number two, and their careers are third. I think that is something that many people, particularly men in management, may not understand—that for those women, their kids are always going to be number one.

As we looked at the careers of these very successful women, we realized that they were not on a "ladder to success." Instead, they were on a stairway to success—a stairway with many landings. They were not necessarily climbing toward the top rapidly at the beginning of their careers, although most had a good start. Instead, they were moving steadily up the stairway, but landing as they needed to due to a childbirth, the needs of their children and families, service to their communities and the profession, as well as the long-term goals they had set for themselves and their teams. They may not have risen to the top quickly like a lot of men do, but they are now on the top, and most have remained there for many years.

They may not have risen to the top quickly like a lot of men do, but they are now on the top, and most have remained there for many years.

One of the women we interviewed is a financial planner who had three babies in her first four years in the business. Her manager said to her, "Nobody can say you're not productive." Fortunately, she found the comment funny, and today one of those children has joined her as a partner in her very successful practice.

Most of the twenty-three women and the top-producing respondents to the survey have left their agencies or corporate offices and have established their own offices. Some have founded their own companies. Several of them talked about how you can't really balance work and family; you have to instead blend them together. Your children and your family need to be a part of your work, and your work needs to be a part of your children and your family. To do that, it was easier for them and their team members to leave the corporate or agency environment or the agency environment and move to their own office space.

Provide Flexible Scheduling as Necessary

As we mentioned earlier, women sometimes require flexibility in scheduling because of their child-care or other commitments outside the office. Conferencing tools like WebEx and FreeConferenceCall.com allow people to participate in meetings from wherever they are—home, the airport, or a satellite office. Everyone doesn't have to be present physically to catch up on what happened yesterday and what they have planned for today. And if someone can't make it, we will catch up with them later. It's not the end of the world.

> *As leaders, we have a unique opportunity to serve as a clearinghouse of resources for our advisors.*

Be a Clearinghouse of Resources

As leaders, we have a unique opportunity to serve as a clearinghouse of resources for our advisors. We can leverage the strength of our firms, agencies, and companies so that our advisors don't have to do everything themselves. The corporate support we offer can help our advisors spend more time in front of clients and less time bogged down with paperwork.

Many women hesitate to admit when they need help. Whereas a man might speak up and say, "Hey, I need some help with this," a woman is likely to keep it to herself, stay up all night to finish, and not say a word. This is true especially if a woman feels like she is in an environment that does not welcome her presence. She may fear that asking for help will make her look incapable of handling the job. A good manager will notice that she needs help and offer it.

There is a tendency for women to try to be Superwoman. Many women feel that they have to excel in all of the roles they play—as a mother, a wife, a professional, a volunteer. We want our advisors to know that we do not expect them to be perfect in everything they do. We can help them learn how to ask for help and delegate work to other people when it's necessary. Delegation is a skill people have to develop. It doesn't come naturally for most people, so that should be a part of our training as well.

Women tend to be caretakers for their families, and they often have personal situations that take up a lot of time and cause them a great deal of anxiety. When there is a challenge in a woman advisor's life, we need to be sensitive to what she is going through and offer the type of flexibility and support that will lighten those burdens. A woman's life issues can be related to a pregnancy, a sick child or parent, or a husband who has a disability, for example. The situation can cause the female advisor to become stressed and unable to focus on her work and clients to the extent she needs to.

In those cases, we can guide women to resources of a more personal nature. For example, many companies have Employee Assistance Programs (EAPs) that offer employees professional and confidential counseling for everything from financial problems to marital issues to a family member struggling with addiction to legal matters. We (Thomasina and team) had a program called LifeWorks at State Farm. Most employees didn't even know about it. When people did use the service—either by calling an 800 number or meeting with a counselor—they thought it was hands-down one of the best benefits that could be offered.

Every one of the twenty-three women who Diane Dixon and Charlie Reed interviewed for their book use teams, both in their offices and in their homes. Charlie says this:

> All of them have put together teams in their offices. They are not lone rangers. Many of the professionals on those teams are people who might be doing planning, investing, or handling insurance operations. They also have teams at home, which are just as important as the teams in their offices. They couldn't do their work without the teams they put together to help them get everything done.

Charlie also says that, when faced with the daunting task of trying to excel in every aspect of their lives, some of the successful women featured in her and Diane's book chose not to advance further in their careers. They opted out of being number one at work so that they could commit more time to their families and charitable work. Charlie tells this story about one of the women she and Diane interviewed:

> One of the women said she realized early on in her career, when she still had young children, that it was possible for her to become number one in her company. She said to her husband, "I think I could do this." And he said, "I know you could do it, but you need to understand that if you do that, you are going to give up all those soccer games you go to and all the charitable work you do." She said that was simply too high of a price to pay. So she settled for being among the top fifty in her company, consistently for thirty years. It wasn't like the other women didn't do the same thing, but they may have done it in different kinds of ways.
>
> It is not that men don't do those same things, but I think it is really surprising to see that with their children being number one, their families being number two, and their careers being number three, these women are still doing all these amazing things in their companies, in the industry, and in their communities. In a couple of cases, they also do a lot also across the world.

Work with a Pregnant Advisor to Create and Carry Out a Maternity Plan

We have mentioned that some managers are reluctant to hire women of child-bearing age. And when a female advisor announces that she is going to have a baby, many managers aren't sure what to do. Diane Dixon suggests that managers help the pregnant advisor figure out a plan for every step of the pregnancy—before, during, and after—to help both her and the firm or agency get all of her work covered. Here is what Diane says:

> I have been coaching full time since 2001, mostly in the financial services industry. Some of the women I have been coaching recently are having their first child. As soon as my business partner and I know that a woman is going to announce her pregnancy at work, we begin to develop her maternity plan. What

is she going to do, and what does she need to be thinking about, when she is five months in? At the sixth month? The seventh month? The eighth month? What's going to happen when she has gone on maternity leave, and what will things look like when she returns to work? We actually build a plan on paper and use it as a working document as the advisor moves through her pregnancy.

> *We actually build a plan on paper and use it as a working document as the advisor moves through her pregnancy.*

Obviously, you don't know exactly when you are going to have the baby and what things are going to be like when the baby arrives, so some of this is just planning. But if you are a woman who is going to go on maternity leave, it is helpful to think this through with your Managing Partner and get his or her feedback and ideas. One Managing Partner asked a female manager how he could help her. He helped cover her coaching during that time because that was important to her. She was delighted, and her respect for him grew even higher. She felt understood.

If you are a Managing Partner, as soon as you find out that one of your advisors or managers is pregnant, offer to help her put together a maternity plan. Or connect the female advisor with somebody who can help her build a good maternity plan so that she is thinking about things that need to happen before she leaves and while she is gone—so she feels respected and cared for.

When women announce they are pregnant, what we want is for our Managing Partners and the other people around us to be excited for us because they are a part of our family too. We want them to be a part of our plan.

Jocelyn Wright says that helping pregnant women navigate the work/life blend will show other women that starting a family doesn't signal the end of their career:

> We need to create an environment where younger women who are thinking about getting married and starting families can see that they can continue in this business. I think teams help with that. We have to create some sort of system where young women think that this is a career for life, not just for a particular period of time in their lives.

Guide Women to Their Ideal Niche Markets

Susan L. Combs suggests using a woman's interest in various causes to help her develop niche markets. Here is what she says:

> I think women do very, very well when they get laser-focused in an area. I always think about it like a past life. A female producer who works for me now used to be a hairdresser. She told me, "Susan, hairdressers are so overlooked when it comes to prospects. All of my hairdresser friends had husbands who made considerable amounts of money, and that is why they could work in a job they love to do."

She started connecting with all of her friends who are hairdressers and talking to them about disability insurance and life insurance; nobody else goes in there and talks to them. So if you look at a woman's past life, you will discover rich opportunities. My own past life involves hospitality, events, and entertainment, so I do a lot of work in the entertainment and food space because I gravitate to that. Like minds enjoy working with like minds.

This is also true of women's volunteer work. If a women is on a board for, say, an association for autistic children, you know there is probably a reason why she is involved in that organization. Maybe she has a child or other family member who is autistic. She can probably develop a niche market with people who have special-needs children. I think it is a great way to set women up for success.

We don't want to sell to our inner circle, and I think a lot of the training models are set up around a producer's "low-hanging fruit." Women do not feel comfortable soliciting our friends and families. So I think we can be more successful at bringing women into our industry if we have them position themselves more as consultants than salespeople. It is all about the positioning. When you bring women in, they are sizing you up because women want to know what is in it for them.

Coach Women Instead of Trying to "Fix" Them

We can support and retain women by taking another look at our culture and our managers' general approach to communicating with women. In many, cases, it seems that managers feel that they have to "fix" a woman because she does not talk or act the way they think she should. They consider her different way of doing things a flaw that needs to be fixed. A better approach is to coach women to be their best and leverage their unique way of doing things.

Diane Dixon shares this story about how she "taught" her Managing Partner to just listen to her instead of trying to "fix" her:

I think back to my Managing Partner; I instructed him along the way. There were times when we would be discussing something, and he would ask me, "Diane, am I fixing or listening this time?"

I would say, "This time you are listening—just listen. Don't try to fix me."

It was great that we got to that place where he would just ask me. I didn't have to say, "I just need you to listen. Just hear me out on this before you respond to anything."

I also had to help him learn how to be aware of differences between the men and me. That is part of teaching people how to treat you and also asking for what you want. When I would win a contest and we would go down to Florida for our trip, the guys wanted to golf all day. That was fine with me, but I didn't want to golf all day. I did one golf event with them because that was always fun. But the rest of the time, I would say, "Dave, what can you do for me instead of golfing?"

He would reply, "Well, go to the beach and rent whatever you need or whatever you want."

In recruiting women, we are trying to open the door to all kinds of possibilities. That ranges from young women who have just graduated from college to mature women who have many life experiences and are seasoned professionals in the fields they worked in during their previous careers.

We also need to grow our advisors from their individual starting points, which can vary a lot among advisors. We need to be respectful of every person's point of entry into this industry. We talked earlier about embracing individuality, and it applies here. It is important that we get to know all of our advisors as individuals and then personalize the support and coaching we provide according to their varying needs.

Encourage Women to Build Strong Relationships with Other Women

Susan L. Combs advises women to maintain at least three strong relationships:

> A woman who owns a coffee company told me a long time ago that at any given time, a woman must have nine deep relationships—three women I am mentoring, three women who are mentoring me, and three peer-to-peer relationships. I am in New York, and we are a little busy to have deep relationships with nine people, but I look to have three deep relationships at all times. I always look to have relationships with people I am helping develop, people who are helping develop me, and a peer.

Understand Differences in Communication Styles

In Chapter 5, we talked about the differences in men's and women's communication styles. It is important for managers to be aware of these differences so that we can communicate effectively with female advisors and managers, as well as female clients. In some cases, it might be helpful to customize your training language to make it resonate with women more.

We realize, however, that the larger your firm or agency is, the more difficult it might be to allow this type of customization. In many cases, the compliance officer in the home office approves the language regarding product training, and the agency or firm is required to use it. Technology can help make basic product training more flexible; advisors can log onto training sites at whatever time is convenient for them.

But in the portions of training that you are allowed to customize—such as when you tell stories to help get the point across—be sensitive about the examples you use. Here are some ways to do that:

1. Avoid telling stories that don't relate to your entire audience, such as those about football, NASCAR, or fishing. Storytelling is a highly effective way to transfer information to people because it helps them retain it. Just be sensitive to your audience, and use inclusive examples that both men and women can relate to.

2. When presenting examples of insurance coverage or investments, don't always refer to a thirty-five-year-old male. Include an example of a twenty-eight-year-old female attorney, for example.

3. When you present a case study, don't always have the man earning more than the woman or being the primary income earner.

4. Deliver your message in a way that ensures that everyone you are training gets it. Presenting different points of view, and inviting discussion, creates a much richer conversation.

And what if you find that some of your compliance office's training materials are not gender-inclusive? Bring it up. Question and challenge it. Collaborate with those in your home office who are providing training materials, and ask them to make the materials more inclusive. Let's use our voice as leaders to help inform and collaborate with our home office partners about this important topic. We want to make sure that we do not use materials in our training sessions that will make women uncomfortable.

Recognize Some Basic Personality Traits of Women

Everyone is different, of course, so we can't say that all women like a certain thing or don't like something else. But there are some significant differences between the genders, generally speaking.

The authors of an October 2015 McKinsey & Company study propose that there is one clear difference between men and women in the United States and most of the world: the amount of power each has in society. They write, "Despite the great strides made in promoting gender equality, women and men don't compete on a level playing field... Women are particularly burdened by prescriptive stereotypes. They are expected to be warm, deferential, and undemanding. This prescriptive stereotype and the double bind it creates limit the ability of women to compete effectively." The authors cite research indicating that both men and women tend to react negatively toward assertive women.[33]

Here are some additional important differences to be aware of.

1. Women Like to Know What to Expect

Women like to be prepared, so when a female advisor and male advisor team up for joint work, it is helpful for them to communicate before going out on client calls. This is especially important when you team up an older, more experienced male advisor with a newer female advisor—she might feel that he is bulldozing over her and leaving her out of the conversation. For those reasons, the advisors should discuss the following before going out on a call:

a. Who will start the discussion with the client, and what will the nature of those comments be?

b. At what point will the second advisor join the conversation, and what will he or she discuss?

---

33 Adam Galinsky and Maurice Schweitzer, "It's Good to be the Queen...But It's Easier to Be the King," McKinsey & Company, October 2015.

c. Review the meeting agenda and decide in advance who will handle which items.

d. Have a predetermined "signal" between advisors so that each one can join the discussion with comment. I (Linda) coached advisors doing joint work to have a special pen or pencil sitting on the desk. If either advisor picked up the pen or pencil casually, it signaled the other advisor to add his or her comments to the discussion. An advisor can also simply say to the other advisor, "Any additional thoughts or comments at this time?"

e. Who will recommend the next step in the process or ask for the sale?

One significant benefit of having male and female advisors team up is that a client might resonate more with one than the other. Train your advisors to "read" your clients' body language. If the client seems to be speaking to the female advisor more, then she probably should take the lead, and the male advisor should take a step back and let that relationship develop. As mentioned above in item "d," have an advance plan to switch "leaders" when the clients' responses indicate this is best.

Another way to help women anticipate what to expect is to use an agenda for client meetings. Having an agenda prepared in advance puts advisors more in control of an appointment. It also makes them look extremely organized and prepared. The agenda doesn't have to be long; it can include just the company logo, the client's name, the date, and the main topics that will be discussed.

2. Women Tend to Be Detail-Oriented

After an appointment, the female advisor and male advisor might have distinctly different ways of summarizing how the call went. As mentioned, most men like to get to the point—the bottom line—right away, while women tend to provide a lot of narrative and lead up to the bottom line. So a woman might be regaling you with all the details about the appointment, and if you are a male, you might get impatient and wonder when she is going to tell you the outcome. We all need to be cognizant of these differences in communication styles. Women need to provide men with the result first, then provide supporting details that are important. And men need to try to be more patient and realize that that is just how women communicate.

If you see female advisors getting overwhelmed with the details, remind them of the *why*—why they are in this business. Encourage them to let the vision of being of service to clients override their insecurities and fear. Ask them to use the adrenaline that's rushing through their veins to propel them forward, as opposed to letting it stop them.

3. Women Ask More Questions than Men

Also, women tend to ask more questions; it's our way of building rapport and educating ourselves about another person's needs. If a female advisor asks a lot of questions in training, be patient with her, and understand that she is just trying to make sure she understands the process.

If you sense that any of your advisors are not fully comfortable with a topic, slow it down. Make sure they will be able to apply the concepts you are teaching them. Ask them to repeat back to you what they think you said. Check their understanding. How ready are the new advisors to go out and present these tools to clients in a confident and effective manner? Have them do role-playing if necessary. Some of the men in the group might not understand the concepts, either, but they are not as likely as women to admit it.

4. Women Often Focus on What They Don't Know

Women's definition of *readiness* tends to differ from men's. With regard to training, asking for a promotion, or just about anything else, men tend to be more comfortable than women with not knowing everything before going into a situation.

Sheryl Sandberg, Chief Operating Officer of Facebook, cites an internal Hewlett-Packard study in her book *Lean In*. The study found that men apply for a job when they consider themselves 60 percent qualified for it, but women won't raise their hands until they feel 100 percent qualified. That goes for even the most ambitious women.

> *Men tend to be more comfortable than women with not knowing everything before going into a situation.*

For example, if a manager mentions a lucrative opportunity in a meeting and asks who wants to be considered, a man is likely to raise his hand immediately and ask to be selected, even if he knows only 60 percent of what he needs to know to do a good job with the endeavor. A woman considers the part she doesn't know to be an obstacle.

Sometimes people hesitate to get involved in an opportunity because they say, "If I knew more, I would do more." Our job as leaders is to encourage people who have great potential to build on that potential, and grow professionally, even if they don't have a high confidence level.

We need to balance women's need to know the details, to be 100 percent ready, and to know what to expect with the need to act in a way that is in our clients' best interest. When we are deep in the discussion about product ideas and investment strategies, it can be very easy to get lost in the details and lose our focus on the reason we are doing all of this—we want to make a difference in people's lives and help them achieve their financial goals.

That focus on what we don't know often leads to fear among women, and that can halt their progress. Part of women's fear is about not knowing the answer to a question a client might ask. When you are training women (and men as well), let them know that they have permission to say, "I don't know, but I will find out and get back to you with the answer soon." In that situation, train them to say to the client, "Now, I want to make sure I understand what you are asking..." People don't care how much you know until they know how much you care. So telling a client, "I don't know, but I will find out" is one more way women can solidify a client relationship. They are showing that they really care about the client's question. And instead of making up an answer or winging it, they care for their client so much that they want to take the time to get the right answer.

There isn't an advisor among us who knows the answer to every single question about financial services today. As leaders, we need to encourage women to get out the door and get started. Motivational speaker Zig Ziglar said, "If you wait until all the lights are green before you leave home, you'll never get started on your trip to the top."

5. Women Sometimes Need Encouragement

One of the things that I (Linda) have found to be a challenge for the women advisors I trained is the emotional stress they feel when they have done all the right things and care very much about the client's best interest, but the client doesn't take their recommendation. Or the client executes part of a plan but not all of it.

Diane Dixon explains how to teach women not to take it personally when a client fails to follow through on her recommendations:

> Women can take this personally when they have built rapport, taken a thorough fact-finder, and put together a wonderful presentation, and the client fails to follow through on the recommendations. We want to remind them that we don't have control over the client's choices. As advisors, our responsibility is to tell the truth and tell it well (i.e., thorough a fact-finder and a clear presentation with spot-on recommendations). The client's responsibility is what he or she ultimately decides to do with those recommendations. I tell our advisors, "The client's lack of follow-through to implement is not on you, and in most instances, it has nothing to do with you or your ability to present."
>
> I would go on to tell a female advisor in this situation, "The relationship you have with your client is a long-term relationship. If you proposed four strategies, and they executed only one of them, then that gives you an agenda for the next three years when you do your annual reviews. You can revisit the recommendations they didn't act on yet." It is important to offer that kind of positive reinforcement when women encounter resistance. It can be easy for them to get discouraged.
>
> We do, however, want to make sure we are asking people to take action. We cannot just present, and because our presentation was excellent and our rapport is off the chart with them, expect that the client will simply sign up. It doesn't work that way. We have to ask people to take action. Remember, many of us grew up being told to be a good girl, do this, don't do that, and it will all work out. You have to ask people to take action in this business.
>
> More than anything, I hear "I don't want to be perceived as pushy. I don't want to be pushy." Well, don't be pushy. Be challenging. Ask your clients, "May I challenge you?" People don't hire you to be their friend; they want an advisor. Take your facts, make your presentation, and at the end—this is what my General Agent taught me—put your pencil down and say, "Is there any reason we can't get started on some or all of this today?" It is that simple. The conversation begins there. If the client says, "I want to think about it," then coach your advisors to respond with this: "Share with me what you really like about what I have shown you so far, and what don't you like. What are you not quite comfortable with?"

You have to ask people to take action in this business.

Get them talking. A lot of times, all the advisor has to do is help facilitate their thinking. Now, you can call that "closing" if you want, but the advisor can also just help them facilitate their thinking and then challenge them to take action. She doesn't have to be pushy and ugly about it; she can simply say, "John, this is really important to you. And these were the recommendations that were made. At this point, you have decided that you are taking no action. There is a big gap between what you said you wanted and what action you are willing to take, and only you can narrow that gap. So what are you going to do to make that gap a little bit smaller? If you are not going to close it all together, okay, but what are you going to do to make it smaller? I don't think zero is the right number."

To me, that is advising and asking for what you want. We want clients to narrow that gap, and they have to decide what they can do.

Emily Viner of Guardian cites recent Guardian research that points to women's reluctance to seem "pushy" as a barrier to sales careers:

> In October 2015, Guardian released a comprehensive study on women in sales. We knew there was an underrepresentation of women in financial services, but what was eye-opening is that it's a bigger challenge than we realized because it is not just about financial services. Really, the bottom line is that women are just not sold on sales...at all—let alone financial services specifically. Women shared their perceptions and stereotypes around sales and salespeople, many of which we all know and cringe at!
>
> Unfortunately, many women think they have to be pushy and highly aggressive to be salespeople—our study showed that 77 percent of women say they are not pushy enough for a sales job. But no one wants to work with a pushy salesperson, and our most successful salespeople are driven by a passion to help people, not push them into a sale. It's frustrating to see this disconnect between what makes a successful salesperson in this business and what women think they need to be in order to be successful. We need to help women see that what they are looking for functionally and emotionally in a career could be met by what a sales career can offer.

One of the best aspects of being in this industry is the fact that we are able to establish long-term—lifelong, in some cases—relationships with our clients. In real estate, you sell someone a home, and it isn't likely that you will sell them another home. But advisors are able to see their clients learn, grow, and reap the rewards of the advisors' recommendations. They can see the clients' children go to college and help them in times of crisis, when there is an insurance claim. That is one of the great things about this career that can really appeal to women, compared to some other selling positions.

A lot of women are slow to accept credit for what they have done well too, so they need managers to recognize them for a job well done. Susan L. Combs sums it up this way:

> Women are kind of horrible at tooting their own horn. So it is helpful if managers

will help women recognize their talent, get them nominated for awards, and help them move up to the next production level. Any kind of recognition goes a long way toward building up a woman's confidence. It could be a formal award, like the WIFS Circle of Excellence recognition, or it can be informal. If a woman in your firm hosted a holiday coat drive for children, announce that on your Facebook page. When you recognize people, they become a billboard for your company. I heard once that when something happens to a woman, she will physically tell an average of thirty-two people, and that has nothing to do with Facebook. When she gets on Facebook, thousands of people will know.

6. Women Like to Tailor the Way They Close a Sale

> *Some of the traditional industry scripts do not allow women to customize the close.*

To grow a successful female advisor, it's important to grow her skills, grow her confidence, and grow her ability to close a sale in her own way. This might mean allowing her to deviate from the usual script a little to make the presentation align more with her personality and selling style.

Some of the traditional industry scripts do not allow women to customize the close. Where possible, allow them to show their clients their respect for their relationship and their understanding of where the client is in the process of executing a recommended financial plan. Allowing women to personalize their closes lets them be sensitive to their relationship with clients.

It is important to role-play this presentation style with women advisors in advance of their client appointments. Don't let them "wing it." Help them gain the confidence they need by mastering their closing style.

Teach Advisors How to Communicate with Women Effectively

Unfortunately, we hear too many stories about advisors who are abrupt, curt, condescending, or downright rude to female clients. Or the advisor will ignore the woman and speak only to her husband.

Research from the Center for Talent Innovation (CTI) found that women do not necessarily prefer a female advisor, but they do expect their advisor to demonstrate gender smarts and exhibit inclusive behaviors. Advisors who create a safe space for questions and candid answers are 56 percent more likely than advisors who don't to forge a satisfactory relationship (56 percent versus 36 percent). And advisors who are sensitive to women's time constraints and manage details women do not have time to attend to are 69 percent more likely than other advisors to build a satisfactory and enduring relationship (61 percent versus 36 percent).[34]

---

34 Sylvia Ann Hewlett and Andrea Turner Moffitt, "The Financial Services Industry's Untapped Market," *Harvard Business Review* website, December 8, 2014, https://hbr.org/2014/12/the-financial-services-industrys-untapped-market.

I (Daralee) have observed women, often in the Traditional generation, make the financial decisions and handle the family finances, but do so secretively. So an advisor might meet with a couple, and the dynamic would be that the husband nods knowingly, and the woman says little, even if she is the one who makes most of the financial decisions for the family. But with our younger generations, these women are less likely to sit there and act like they don't know anything. They will expect respect and acknowledgment as decision makers.

My (Linda's) mother passed away six years ago. She always handled the family finances. She was one of those people who balanced the checkbook within one penny. Long after I was out of college and I had just started this career in the early 1980s, I met with my parents. My mother said, "Now that you kids are out of college, we really want to save more money for retirement." And my dad said, "Oh, honey, I don't think we have any money to do that." She replied, "Yes, we are going to do that." So my dad, who is a retired pastor and now ninety-two years old, started not only IRAs, but he was able to start a TSA, which is the nonprofit equivalent of a 401(k). He funded it to the max for years and years. He had more money in retirement savings than he ever imagined he could accumulate in his entire lifetime just because my mom put her foot down and said, "We are saving for retirement." That is my mother's legacy.

But despite the overwhelming evidence that women are often the financial decision makers, we know that many women feel that financial advisors treat them in a condescending way.

According to a 2012 study titled "Women of Wealth," women are convinced that "their gender is a key factor in the disrespect and condescension they encounter." And all of the women polled for this survey by the Family Wealth Advisors Council—a network of wealth-management firms—had a net worth of greater than $1 million, so their treatment wasn't due to coming in with puny portfolios.[35]

I (Daralee) have seen women leave their prior broker because of how they had been treated. Often the offending behavior involves not offering explanations about the specifics of the recommendations and just expecting the client to implement blindly. Women reasonably expect explanations, and with enough questions asked, that advice must be tailored to their specifics.

Often the offending behavior involves not offering explanations about the specifics of the recommendations and just expecting the client to implement blindly.

Recently, I (Daralee) was interviewed for an article that appeared in *InvestmentNews*.[36] It discussed how advisors help female clients create a legacy and accomplish what they want with their wealth.

It is a wise financial advisor who focuses on this area. Because women often live longer than men and often live alone toward the end of their lives, it is important to prioritize having their legacies carried out. About 70 percent of female clients leave their financial

---

35   Kerry Hannon, "Women and Financial Advisors: A Rocky Relationship," May 15, 2012, NextAvenue website, http://www.nextavenue.org/women-and-financial-advisers-rocky-relationship/.

36   Liz Skinner, "Tools for Legacy Planning to Help Clients—And Hold On to Their Inheritors," August 10, 2015, *InvestmentNews* website, http://www.investmentnews.com/article/20150810/FREE/150819996/tools-for-legacy-planning-to-help-clients-and-hold-on-to-their.

advisor within a year of their husband's death, due to avoidable disconnect.[37]

As I said to *InvestmentNews*, if we lose the business of a single beneficiary when a client dies, that is a big deal to us. We don't take it lightly because if we are going to be of service to our clients and protect their assets, we have to be in touch with the beneficiaries and establish ourselves as their resource. We can be the voice of those clients and help them carry their legacy forward. Women frequently have a vision that extends beyond themselves. Female advisors can be well suited here, with their natural tendency to relate.

We can make a difference. By helping women with their finances and providing more assistance in the area of legacy, they can build a relationship with a financial advisor that is based on trust. They do not want to be talked down to, dismissed, or told, in essence, "Buy this product and go away."

> *It is important for advisors to pay equal attention to male and female clients.*

It is important for advisors to pay equal attention to male and female clients, listen to their concerns, check their understanding of those concerns, and offer solutions that are appropriate for the situation.

Sallie Krawcheck, former president of the global wealth management division of Bank of America, offers these tips for doing a better job of attracting and retaining female clients:

1. Talk with women, not at them.

2. Focus on risk. Women value wealth preservation seven times more than they value upside risk.

3. Frame investing around goals. Women care more about whether or not they can send their children to college than they do about how their portfolio did versus the stock market last year.[38]

Teach Advisors How Women and Men Invest Differently

It's also important for advisors to understand how women's perspectives on investing differ from men's.

Both men and women view wealth as a source of financial security and independence. But once these priorities are met, women look to leverage their wealth to provide a larger basket of goods for themselves, their families, and, importantly, for society at large. In the CTI study we mentioned earlier, US women are 27 percent more likely than men to want to invest in organizations that promote social well-being. And, while women seek good portfolio performance, they also look for an advisor relationship that is grounded in communication and trust. They want their advisor to include them in the investing process and to make it clear how their investments align with their interests and life goals.[39]

---

37 Kristan Wojnar and Chuck Meek, "Women's Views of Wealth and the Planning Process: It's Their Values That Matter, Not Just Their Value," *Advisor Perspectives*, March 2011, https://nationalfinancial.fidelity.com/app/literature/view?itemCode=9586691&renditionType=pdf.

38 "Women: An $11 Trillion Market for Financial Advisors?" June 25, 2015, CNBC website, http://www.cnbc.com/2015/06/25/women-an-11-trillion-market-for-financial-advisors.html.

39 "The Financial Service's Industry's Untapped Market," ibid.

As part of the 2013 Insights on Wealth and Worth, US Trust surveyed high-net-worth women across the country to better understand their perspective and behavior related to wealth and wealth management. Here are some of the study's key findings:

1. Sixty-two percent of women compared to 76 percent of men feel financially secure about the future. Of women who don't feel financially secure, their top concern is having enough income in retirement.

2. Nearly two-thirds (63 percent) of women say asset growth is a higher investment priority than asset protection.

3. Women are nearly twice as likely as men to say that giving to charity is the most satisfying aspect of having wealth.

4. Nearly four in ten women (39 percent) have forfeited income or advancement of their careers to care for the special needs of children or parents.

5. Women are less likely than men to have important financial documents and estate-planning tools in place. More than three-quarters (78 percent) of women do not have a comprehensive estate plan, 36 percent do not have a will, 51 percent have not named a health proxy, and 66 percent have not named a durable power of attorney.[40]

Charlie Reed says many of the female clients she works with like to take their time making financial decisions:

> In general, women need to have a stronger understanding of something before we are willing to act on it, and that is something I think the industry has to really look at carefully. I think that is true of women consumers too, and I don't think the industry has figured that out. Women consumers are not willing to just take the advice of an advisor. They may be willing at some point when they really trust that person, but when they are just starting out in their own financial planning, they really want to understand something before they are going to purchase it or before they are going to go in a particular direction with their financial plan. I think that is important for management to know about women.

From your own experience in this industry, you can build your own repository of data about the differences between men and women investors. The genders differ in their perspectives about money, their methods of investing, and their priorities. Use this treasure trove of insight to create a training program for advisors that will educate them about how to work effectively with clients of both genders.

You can build your own repository of data about the differences between men and women investors.

---

40   US Trust/Bank of America, "Women and Wealth Fact Sheet," 2013, http://www.ustrust.com/publish/content/application/pdf/GWMOL/ARS7ME57.pdf.

How Some Companies Are Supporting Women

With a little creativity, you can come up with innovative strategies for training women—and helping men and women work together effectively. Here are some examples of strategies that a few financial services firms are using to support their female staff members:

1. Goldman Sachs conducts regularly scheduled get-togethers in which the firm's senior leadership, top female wealth advisors, and female advisors newer to the business compare notes, swap stories, and make connections.

2. US Trust is developing a "boot camp" for advisors that will arm them with a more comprehensive understanding and passion for tapping into the female investor market.

3. Charles Schwab formed a Women's Advisory Council to help advisors understand and respond to the rising opportunity presented by working with female investors.[41]

4. Many firms, such as Met Life, AIG, Guardian, Penn Mutual, New York Life, Thrivent, and Raymond James have women's initiatives aimed at recruiting and supporting women.

Here are some of our additional tips for supporting female advisors:

1. Training and support aren't just for new advisors. Most women enjoy having the chance to constantly improve their skills and better themselves. By providing ongoing support and training to all female advisors, you will enable them to learn new skills, take on more responsibility, and possibly be promoted into management.

2. You don't have to have a trainer in your firm or agency; you can have your third- or fourth-year advisors—or veteran advisors—provide valuable tips to first-year advisors, either in a joint-work situation or in speaking at a training class.

3. Mentoring is a key element of support as well. A female advisor's mentor doesn't have to be another female; a male can be just as effective a mentor. We talk more about mentoring in Chapter 10, "Women Growing Women."

As we said earlier, gender diversity doesn't stop at recruiting. Once you attract quality women into your organization, build in every type of support necessary to ensure that they thrive.

---

41   Hewlett and Moffitt, "The Financial Services Industry's Untapped Market."

Questions to Ask Yourself

1. To what extent would technology help you provide flexibility in scheduling meetings? Consider using tools like WebEx and FreeConferenceCall.com to allow advisors to participate in meetings without physically being in the office.

2. Do you have a list of resources that would be helpful for advisors, both in terms of their careers and their personal lives? Make a list of agency or firm, company, and community resources, and have it ready to give to an advisor who might need support.

3. Does your compliance office require you to follow scripts for product presentations and other conversations with clients? If so, are they gender-neutral? If they are not, how likely are you to mention it to your home office? If you are not required to follow company guidelines, to what extent do you need to revise your materials to make them appropriate for both female and male advisors to use?

4. To what extent does your training program prepare female advisors to excel in the career? What can you do to enhance your training? Which of your veteran advisors or product specialists can you ask to make presentations to newer advisors?

5. Do you use joint work in your firm or agency? If not, why not consider pairing up female advisors with male advisors so that clients have a more well-rounded experience?

CHAPTER 9

Promoting Successful Women into Leadership

"In a world that favors leadership based on skills of personal interaction rather than on authority, women have a head start."
—Geoff Colvin,
Fortune Senior Editor-at-Large

In Chapter 1, we mentioned that only 25.7 percent of the financial advisors in the United States are women. At the management level, that percent drops considerably. Numbers from the Center for American Progress show that in the financial services industry, only 12.4 percent of executive officers in 2014 were women, and 18.3 percent of board directors were women. According to their numbers, no CEOs were women.[42]

Not all leaders look, act, or manage the same way. Some people might think that the most effective leader is the in-your-face, aggressive, brash man who can make a riveting presentation in front of a large group. But that leader might be terrible at one-on-one communication, mentoring, and providing personalized support to advisors as they need it. A more reserved woman who does not excel at motivational speaking can be just as effective a leader and highly effective at nurturing and mentoring individuals, recognizing potential, noticing who needs support, and providing it.

In this chapter, we offer advice to women about how to move into leadership, as well as tips for men who want to promote women in their agencies, firms, and companies into management.

Barriers That Prevent Women from Entering Management

Theories vary regarding the reasons women are not considered for management in our industry. We think one reason is that because of prevailing stereotypes, women simply are not considered as managerial candidates when it is time to promote someone. Women are simply overlooked.

I (Thomasina) think part of the reason we haven't seen the kind of change we thought we would see by this time is because the folks at the very top are delegating down to their managers, saying, "You need to go out and hire more women." But most people look up and see no women in the C-suite or in the executive office. If people see that you have surrounded yourself with men, but you are telling your managers to hire more women,

---

42 Judith Warner, "Fact Sheet: The Women's Leadership Gap," March 7, 2014, Center for American Progress website, https://www.americanprogress.org/issues/women/report/2014/03/07/85457/fact-sheet-the-womens-leadership-gap/.

> *You have to start including women at the higher levels, where you are, or it doesn't look like you believe in the message.*

then you are not walking the talk. We just need to pull the veil off and call it what it is. You can't dictate *down* what has to happen. You have to start including women at the higher levels, where you are, or it doesn't look like you believe in the message.

According to a 2014 Caliper study, the top five barriers female leaders experienced were as follows. Three of them relate to work/life balance, while only two relate to workplace issues:

1. Feelings of guilt for not spending enough time with family because of work
2. Family responsibilities interfering with work
3. Resistance from other current leaders
4. Having to outperform male leaders to be considered effective
5. Lack of support in the household when work is demanding[43]

The Caliper study also took a close look at "stereotype threat," which is a common barrier to women's success in management. This phenomenon occurs when a member of a group engages in an activity or performs a task for which a negative stereotype about the group exists. As a result, the individual may have anxiety about being judged or treated stereotypically. Research suggests that the presence of this threat may subconsciously lead people to underperform and conform to the very stereotypical behaviors they were trying to avoid.[44]

The study adds that most women are aware of leadership and gender-role stereotypes that typically favor men. So they often react to the stereotype threat by adopting more masculine behaviors and communication styles. And that is usually counterproductive for women. When women leaders adopt a more masculine style in response to stereotype threat, they are rated as less warm by their subordinates, and the people they supervise are less willing to comply with the requests of the women leaders when compared to male leaders who made the same requests.[45]

Jocelyn Wright of The American College has seen this phenomenon firsthand—women acting masculine to fit into a male-dominated culture. She encourages women to be proud of their feminine qualities:

> I spoke with a young advisor recently who works in an office that employs only one other woman. She said she felt like she had to kind of "man up" to fit in. So she didn't dress or act very feminine, and she wouldn't wear bright colors. I told her she shouldn't feel like she had to act masculine to fit into a male-dominated office. Unfortunately, she has left the industry, but I think that happens far too often.

43 "Women Leaders," Caliper Research Paper, December 2014, available for download at https://www.calipercorp.com/home-3/banner-women-leaders-white-paper/.
44 Ibid.
45 Ibid.

We should feel free to be feminine and to exhibit the qualities that are generally inherent in women and make us unique—those caring and compassionate qualities, the ability to listen and relate to individuals, and that more attuned sense of communication that is important when we work with clients. Just because we work in a largely male-dominated field, we should not feel like we have to mask our femininity. If we do, we are not serving ourselves, we are not serving our clients, and if we are working in an environment or in a team with other men, we are not serving them, either, because we bring something very unique to the table, and that certainly helps enhance teams.

First the "Glass Ceiling," Then the "Glass Cliff"

When we promote women into leadership, we want to set them up to succeed. A lot of factors impact a manager's success. So as you are promoting women into leadership positions, think about the positions you are putting them in, and think about the challenge of those positions relative to what is going on in the organization.

We have all heard of the "glass ceiling," which refers to the fact that women often rise to a certain level in an organization and then hit the proverbial "glass ceiling" and cannot progress any farther up the hierarchy. A more recent barrier that has been documented for women is called the "glass cliff." Psychology professors Michelle Ryan and Alex Haslam discovered this phenomenon, in which women are more likely than men to be put into leadership roles under risky and precarious circumstances. By taking the helm in difficult times, their odds of failure are often higher.

Women are more likely than men to be put into leadership roles under risky and precarious circumstances.

Research over the past decade has documented the "glass cliff." One reason women are given these more challenging leadership opportunities, studies say, is that there is a common belief that men possess qualities that are more of a fit with running successful companies, while women possess qualities that can make them more suitable in difficult situations. When asked to describe managers in successful companies, people tend to list more stereotypical masculine qualities such as "decisive" and "forceful." But when asked how desirable different characteristics were for managers of unsuccessful companies, the number of stereotypical female qualities (such as "intuitive" and "understanding") outweighed the number of masculine traits. These kinds of findings have led some people to conclude that when we think crisis, we think female.[46]

On first glance, it might seem that having all this confidence in women to solve crises is a compliment to our gender—but this situation sets women up to fail. Despite inheriting problems, women in glass-cliff positions are often held fully responsible for the bad state of affairs. This dynamic also can reinforce stereotypes and cultural beliefs that men are better leaders in the first place.[47]

---

46 Marianne Cooper, "Think Crisis—Think Female: Why Women Leaders Confront the Glass Cliff," LinkedIn, September 15, 2015, https://www.linkedin.com/pulse/think-crisis-female-why-women-leaders-confront-glass-cliff-cooper.
47 Ibid.

A few years ago, we (Linda and team) had a new female advisor who was a dynamo—she was very successful. She was promoted into management, which meant she had to grow new advisors in a different location, moving with her husband and infant daughter to another state. She ultimately left the organization in tears. In retrospect, I think we pushed her too far, too fast, and we put her in a situation in which she was not likely to succeed. A male manager would not have done any better in this situation. To increase her odds for success, I think she needed more time to be mentored where she was, where she had her network and knew everybody, before she moved. Maybe we should have tried out a transitional arrangement, where she would work as a middle manager half the time and still work with her clients half the time. She gave up her entire client base to move to a new state.

In these situations, we have to balance the organization's best interest with the individual's best interest. Whose needs are we putting first?

This is why we need to be cognizant about moving people—both men and women—into certain markets and certain environments. Regardless of gender, we need to make sure the person has the skills, experience, personality, drive, and support to excel in the new position. And once they are in the new position, we need to interact with them often to find out how the transition is going and get their feedback. It is our job to support them in any way that's necessary. Part of that support is to help them transition out of a new opportunity if it doesn't work out. That will help diffuse the fear that might keep someone from considering a new challenge.

> *Failure is not death; it is just one situation that didn't work out.*

I (Thomasina) like to say that failure is not death; it is just one situation that didn't work out. It doesn't help the company in the long run if we put people in new positions and they fail. If we get this right for women, we will get it right for everybody.

Traits of Successful Women Managers

Knowing traits that are common among successful female leaders gives us something to look for as we're considering females for the management role.

Caliper researchers recently found six personality traits of women managers at the senior vice president level or higher that were associated with higher performance ratings:

1. **Assertiveness:** Being straightforward in her communication style

2. **Aggressiveness:** Bringing in a constructive, emotional element to move projects forward

3. **Empathy:** Being able to understand and relate to the feelings of others

4. **Ego strength:** Being resilient and able to overcome challenges

5. **Stress tolerance:** Being comfortable in high-stress environments

6. **Energy:** Bringing vitality and enthusiasm to her work[48]

---

48 Jenna Goudreau, "Six Personality Traits of High-Performing Women," January 21, 2015, *Business Insider* website, http://www.businessinsider.com/personality-traits-of-high-performing-women-2015-1.

Caliper concluded that a woman who has a straightforward communication style, is resilient and able to handle stress, and is able to relate to others may be best positioned for leadership success in the modern workplace.[49] Look for these traits in the women you know.

Gallup recently conducted thousands of interviews in all types of organizations, at all levels, and in almost all industries. The results showed that employees felt female managers were more likely to encourage employee development than their male counterparts. The Gallup research revealed twelve elements of management style that tend to predict the *engagement* level of employees, as well as the level of employee and work-group performance. Employees of female managers outscored employees of male managers on eleven of the twelve items. Gallup found that employees who work for female managers in the United States are more engaged than those who work for male managers.[50]

> *A woman who has a straightforward communication style, is resilient and able to handle stress, and is able to relate to others may be best positioned for leadership success in the modern workplace.*

A Step-by-Step Process for Promoting Women

Given all of those statistics, it is difficult to argue about women's efficacy as managers. So how do we turn the tide and promote more women into management? Women matter in your frontline sales force, and they matter in leadership.

A Women's Leadership Study that KPMG conducted in 2015 found that, to empower more women to reach the highest ranks of leadership, we must focus on three key areas: socializing leadership early in life, modeling leadership and building confidence through role models and networking, and providing or enhancing corporate-development programs that move more women forward.[51]

The study provided these five recommendations for increasing gender diversity among management teams:

1. Identify and develop those high-performing women who aspire to lead.

2. Provide the kind of individual feedback that reinforces and builds confidence and high performance.

3. Build empowered and effective networks with the express goal of generating opportunities for women's leadership growth.

4. Actively give qualified women leadership opportunities.

5. Put in place challenging and aspirational career paths for women at work.

---

49 Ibid.

50 Kimberly Fitch and Sangeeta Agrawal, "Why Women Are Better Managers than Men," October 16, 2014, Gallup website, http://www.gallup.com/businessjournal/178541/why-women-better-managers-men.aspx.

51 "KPMG Women's Leadership Study: Moving Women Forward into Leadership Roles," 2015, KPMG website, https://www.kpmg.com/US/en/IssuesAndInsights/ArticlesPublications/Documents/womens-leadership-study.pdf.

We have created our own step-by-step process for increasing the number of females in management in agencies and firms.

1. Hire female advisors with leadership potential

It can start as early as during the advisor selection process. Always look to identify candidates who have great leadership potential. If we let a candidate know we might want to consider her for management roles at some point in the future, that might make her more inclined to join the agency or firm, first as an advisor.

In this situation, we need to let women know that the timing is flexible, and we will not promote them until both they and we feel they are ready. We can create mentorship arrangements and joint-work opportunities and let them proceed at a pace that is comfortable to them. It should be a very deliberate decision to move into management, for both the manager who is encouraging that move and the person who is considering it.

It is important to have this open dialogue with a woman about her leadership potential early on and not have it be a one-way conversation, as in, "We want you to move to another region next month and manage thirty people."

2. Approach women with management potential

We need to tap women on the shoulder and say, "I think you would be an excellent candidate for a management role."

Often, we need to tap women on the shoulder and say, "I think you would be an excellent candidate for a management role." Men are pretty quick to raise their hands, whether they are prepared for the position or not, but many women need to be approached. We mentioned earlier that men are more likely to vie for an opportunity if they are only 60 percent qualified, whereas women won't think they should be considered unless they are 100 percent ready. So as leaders, we need to be keen observers of people's potential. And we need to avoid being biased by someone's family situation to decide that she shouldn't be considered for a promotion.

I (Linda) was blessed by support very early in my career from Karsten Lundring. He gave me opportunities to gain confidence while I was an advisor by having me do the following:

1. Make presentations at meetings on a specific product idea or successful strategy.

2. Teach occasional classes for new advisors.

3. Make joint field appointments with new advisors.

After I moved into a frontline leader role, my first task was to recruit someone to replace me to serve my clients. It was natural for me to hire a woman to replace myself, and I was very comfortable training her with joint appointments with my clients. She got an excellent career start, and I felt satisfied that my clients were being well cared for. Best of all, that first experience as a new frontline manager gave me the confidence that I could recruit and train successfully.

In addition, Karsten connected me with various volunteer leadership roles—serving on the board of a local nursing home and on the GAMA International board of directors. In both of these volunteer capacities, I gained experience and confidence and eventually became president of the board of both organizations.

Karsten's encouragement and ability to make connections for me with these opportunities made a tremendous difference in my development as a woman in this industry. I would challenge each of us to follow this example.

3. Show them what management entails

Not every advisor wants to be a manager—in fact, many of them are downright critical of anyone who does consider management. Many times, the most successful advisors are the least likely to consider management. They do not understand why anybody would want to be a manager when, as advisors, they have such great control over their personal space, their practices, and their income potential. On their own, they can immediately impact whatever it is they need to do. But the concept of getting results and making an impact through others is foreign to them. So not everybody finds that role appealing.

But getting work done through others is an extremely valuable skill. In March 2015, *Fortune* magazine named fifteen women as the World's Greatest Leaders. The one trait they all shared? The ability "to influence a wide range of groups over which they have no direct authority." *Fortune* Senior Editor-at-Large Geoff Colvin writes, "Extensive research shows how women are better suited to this kind of leadership. They're better than men at empathy—sensing the thoughts and feelings of others and responding in some appropriate way. They value reciprocal relationships more highly than men do."[52]

Having potential managers shadow other managers, either male or female, is one way to let them see what a manager's day-to-day functions are really like. Consider a "reverse mentor" role too. Ask a person who is thinking of a leadership role to be a mentor to a brand-new advisor. Ask her to go out and do some field training and help the new advisor. Let her see what it feels like to get work done through others, to see what it feels like to make a difference in the life of another advisor, the same way she feels satisfaction about making a difference in the lives of her clients.

Having potential managers shadow other managers, either male or female, is one way to let them see what a manager's day-to-day functions are really like.

4. Help women develop managerial skills

As women gain experience as advisors, encourage them to complete professional certifications, learn new product lines, and get experience with a wide variety of clients. Encourage them to develop all types of skills, from public speaking to delegation to coaching. Teach them what you have learned as the most valuable managerial skills. Share

---

52 Geoff Colvin, "The Trait That Makes Women Great Leaders," March 26, 2015, *Fortune* website, http://fortune.com/2015/03/26/the-trait-that-makes-women-great-leaders/.

with them your successes as well as your challenges. These firsthand experiences will be valuable to them, and it will put them at ease to know that you didn't do everything perfectly the first time you tried it. No one does.

5. Allow women to transition into management slowly

It is helpful in many situations to allow people to transition into management slowly, to let them "dip their toes" into management without leaving the advisor role completely. If they move into the new role abruptly and giving up their entire book of business, only to find that they are not happy in management, it is likely be a traumatic experience for them.

6. Provide ongoing support

With any newly promoted manager, it is important to check in regularly to find out what is going well, what could be improved, and how we, as leaders, can help.

In our industry, we are fortunate that GAMA International (www.gamaweb.com) offers myriad resources for managers. GAMA's website allows someone who is contemplating leadership to read issues of the *GAMA International Journal* and other resources, work on self-study programs, attend the annual LAMP conference to learn from other leaders, and find a mentor to shadow, either in their own company or in another company.

A woman's mentor can be either male or female, and the mentor can be in another industry as well. Leadership is leadership, and field training is field training. Regardless of where she shadows a manager, it will be a safe space in which a female manager can learn critical skills from someone who is doing the job every day. Just watching the strength and fortitude a female leader brings to the marketplace every day is a valuable learning experience that she can't find in any classroom or video.

Female managers can establish their own personal board of directors— influential people from inside or outside the industry.

Similarly, female managers can establish their own personal board of directors—influential people from inside or outside the industry. A female manager can ask her board of directors for ideas, suggestions, and feedback. She can ask the members of her board to complete a survey for her periodically, rating her on a scale from 1 to 5 in areas like how coachable she is, how well she coaches others, and how likely others are to follow her lead.

In the next chapter, "Women Supporting Women," we provide tips for ways in which established female managers can support new female managers.

7. Encourage leadership

Later in this chapter, Thomasina mentions the concept of changing an organization from the inside. Women are often motivated to help facilitate change because it is the right thing to do, and in our business, everything we do benefits other people. So the better our companies are, the better we are, and the better service we provide to our clients.

We need to encourage women to look for areas in our agencies and firms that could be changed for the better. Wouldn't it be better to change those areas from the inside than from the outside, diving in? The possibility of being a change agent appeals to most women, and this is one way to motivate advisors to consider becoming managers.

8. Help build their confidence

We do not want to suggest that all women lack confidence, but some do, especially if they are considering a role that is new and unfamiliar to them. A woman might have the skills she needs, but she might need help developing a "thicker skin" to deal with those who think she is not qualified for management just because she is a woman.

I (Thomasina) believe most women can handle rejection in sales. They typically don't take that personally. But I have seen some situations in which women were criticized for attempting management. In one situation, a male manager told a woman who I think was absolutely one of the most talented managers in the company that she didn't have enough presence to be in management. The comments were completely false and were demoralizing to her.

We need to prepare women for that type of rejection and help them build enough confidence to look people like that in the eye and say, "You may not think I am qualified, but I do." Unfortunately, I got that kind of confidence in spades, so I don't ever have that problem. But I have worked with so many women who have experienced comments like that. I just wish I could make them into a "hard-boiled egg" so that some of those comments didn't get to them and cause them to become emotionally distressed.

If I (Daralee) sense fear in new managers, I tell them that they will be working with people, just like they work with clients as an advisor. Their role is to support and be a resource. And just like they never know what a client is going to do or say, they will never be able to predict what they will encounter as managers. In thirty-three years in this business, I have never had a day that was predictable. Every day has surprises. And that is the beauty of this business.

Managers focus on increasing productivity by controlling activity and numbers. *Leaders* elevate someone to a level of confidence that they don't have to focus on that control. To grow, you have to let go. Through leadership, we will get where we need to go. We are not going to manage our way to serving today's marketplace. So when we are recruiting females, instead of trying to control them, we should focus on things leaders can do to empower the women in their organizations to grow into leadership over time.

How the Authors Became Managers

The three authors of this book had different experiences in terms of moving from the advisor role into management. We want to share them with you so that you can see how promoting women into management can be a natural process.

Daralee's Experience

I got into leadership accidentally. When I was an advisor, I brought other people into the firm. I created a little team. I was mentoring them and doing joint work with them. I didn't know any of these processes had names at that time. I just knew that there were more clients than I could personally get to, and I needed to bring in family and friends to help me with this noble mission of bringing financial security and planning to people. That is when my mentor said, "You really should be a manager; you are already doing it." I didn't realize I was managing, but that is exactly what I was doing.

Linda's Experience
When I was an advisor at Thrivent, our leader was Karsten Lundring, as I've mentioned. At organization meetings, he would ask advisors to present case studies of cases that worked well, especially with new products when they came out. Because I had a teaching background, I really loved doing that, and I was asked to present several times. It fit in well with my teaching background, and I really enjoyed it, so my enthusiasm showed through. I had a chance to show some leadership in that regard while I was still an advisor.

Then the organization launched a new program and hired additional middle managers. I was one of the logical choices because I had already shown this leadership talent in terms of presenting and also training, which was what they wanted new middle managers to do. Karsten, being the kind of leader he is, wanted gender equality among leadership teams, so he worked to have me be his co-Managing Partner.

Thomasina's Experience
I was one of the first African American female agents to be selected in the middle Tennessee area. So in all of my training classes, I was the only woman, and one of only a few minorities. I would bug all the managers about when they were going to change that so that I would have some people to hang out with at meetings. They wouldn't pay me any attention. I finally decided that I needed to be in management, so I started raising my hand. Well, people laughed at me. There weren't a whole lot of people like me around saying they wanted to go into management.

I actually had a problem from both sides. One time, I went to a meeting of African American agents. This guy stood up and said, "I heard that there is this black female agent who wants to become a manager, and I don't know why she would want to do something that stupid. The white men don't even want to be managers."

I stood up and said, "That would be me you're talking about, and let me just tell you, I think it takes a lot more courage to change things from the inside than it does to stand on the outside and talk about it."

I would get on the phone and just kept calling everybody. I heard Georgia was going to be a new territory for State Farm, and I found out who was going to be in charge. I kept calling him and telling him I was interested. I told him, "You really need to talk to me because I am going to be the best thing you ever hired." He finally gave me an interview, and the rest is history.

Now that you know the traits of successful female managers, common barriers that prevent women's entry into management, and some practical steps to promoting women, we hope that the next time you are looking to fill a managerial position, you will consider one of your female advisors.

Questions to Ask Yourself

1. In your firm or agency, have you ever promoted, or considered promoting, a woman into management? How well did it work out? If it worked out well, what factors contributed to her success? If it did not work out well, what factors contributed to her failure? What could you, as a leader, have done differently to achieve a better outcome?

2. Are you looking to promote someone into management right now? If so, are you considering any women for the role? If not, why not?

3. What traits would a woman need for you to consider her for a management role? How do those traits differ from those you would require of a male manager?

4. If advisors whom you would like to promote do not find the management role appealing, how much do they really know about management? What can you do to educate them about a manager's most important responsibilities—and the rewards that go with them?

CHAPTER 10

Women Growing Women

"I have always believed that one woman's success can only help another woman's success."

—Gloria Vanderbilt

In Chapter 8, we discussed ways in which all managers, both male and female, can support female advisors and managers. In this chapter, we provide strategies that women managers can employ to increase the chances of success for female advisors and managers we recruit into our organizations.

> *Because women tend to thrive on collaboration, we share a special affinity for sharing information with one another.*

Because women tend to thrive on collaboration, we share a special affinity for sharing information with one another. One of the best ways to connect with other women is to tell a story about a personal situation from your own experience to show them that they are not alone. The key is to engage with them as individuals.

Here are some specific tips that women can use to "grow" women to their optimum potential in this industry.

Encourage Women to Learn from One Another

Women in Insurance & Financial Services (WIFS), the preeminent professional organization for women in the insurance and financial services industry, "is dedicated to *attracting* capable women to the insurance and financial services sector, *developing* their talents, and *advancing* them toward their fullest potential."[53]

WIFS offers myriad networking opportunities, including a national conference, social media interaction, a speakers' bureau, and local events in dozens of chapters across the country. Educational resources include webinars, videos, articles, and frequent sharing of career tips. And, through the WIFS mentoring program, veteran members guide women who are seeking to launch, re-engage, or ignite their careers.

Women need to seek each other out and share best practices and lessons learned. As members of industry organizations like GAMA International, NAIFA, MDRT, FPA, study groups, and others, women need to seek out other women and use the groups as a networking opportunity

---

53 "Our Mission," Women in Financial Services website, https://wifsnational.org/.

Provide a Mentoring Program

As we mentioned in the previous chapter, an aspiring female manager's mentor can be either a man or a woman. Some companies establish their own mentoring programs; others take advantage of established programs.

MDRT Mentoring Program

One of the most respected mentoring programs in our industry is the Million Dollar Round Table (MDRT) Mentoring Program.

The program is designed for newer agents. Mentees, or "aspirants," as MDRT calls them, may not participate if they have had more than one year of MDRT membership. More experienced agents who worry that spending time with aspirants[54] will reduce their productivity have no need to worry. A recent MDRT analysis of 2013 production for 2014 membership shows that, on average, US MDRT members participating in the MDRT Mentoring Program experienced an increase in qualifying commission of $23,000 and $123,000 in qualifying premium over their 2012 production.

A Mentoring Program for Women Only

The MDRT program is for both men and women, but the Mentoring Women's Network is dedicated to women. The group pairs female mentors with female mentees and offers individual as well as corporate mentoring programs. According to the organization's website, a five-year study found that mentees are 40 percent more likely to be promoted, and their mentors are 50 percent more likely to be promoted.[55]

> *You can pair newer advisors or agents with more senior females in a mentoring relationship without creating an elaborate program.*

Tips for Establishing Your Own Mentoring Program

You can pair newer advisors or agents with more senior females in a mentoring relationship without creating an elaborate program. Just make sure the mentoring effort is built around a structured process, or it's not likely to take off. How many times have people asked us to be their mentor, and we agree, and then nothing happens? Once two people agree to engage in a mentoring relationship, we recommend that they decide on the following procedure to help ensure the success of the relationship:

1. First, it's important for the mentee to seek out a mentor who has the skills and experience she needs help with. The more specific her goals are, the more likely it is that the mentorship will be a success. A goal might be to gain confidence with public speaking or to learn delegation tips.

2. Once both parties determine that the mentor and mentee are a good fit, they need to discuss, and then put in writing, what both parties hope to accomplish, in specific

---

54 "About Mentoring," MDRT website, https://www.mdrt.org/membership/mentoring/.
55 Mentoring Women's Network website, http://mentoringwomensnetwork.com/. You can sign up for the MWN newsletter at http://mentoringwomensnetwork.com/news-letter/.

terms, and within what time frame. For example: "The mentee hopes to define a career path within six meetings."

3.   Discuss the best days and times to meet, and decide on a regular meeting time— maybe the first and third Thursday of every month from 10:00 to 11:00 a.m.

4.   Decide in advance what to discuss during each meeting, and create an agenda for each meeting.

5.   After each mentoring meeting, write and save a brief summary of what was discussed and key takeaways. Once the mentoring sessions are completed, both parties will have a summary of all the tips the mentor provided to the mentee. This summary might be useful in future mentoring partnerships or in training.

> *After each mentoring meeting, write and save a brief summary of what was discussed and key takeaways.*

Why Women Have Difficulty Finding Mentors

A 2014 *Forbes* article reports that women have a more difficult time than men finding mentors. One reason is that those women who are both leaders and had family responsibilities are the ones mentees most want to emulate, but they were also are those who have the least time to mentor.

A second reason is that many women are reluctant to ask for mentors, even when they want them.

A third reason is females who sabotage other females' success. (We listed this unfortunate type of scenario as Pothole #8 in Chapter 3 of this book.) "Queen Bees" are career women who not only have zero interest in fostering the careers of other women, but they may actively attempt to cut them off at the pass. The *Forbes* article said, "Queen Bees exist largely as a result of a still-patriarchal work culture in which comparatively few women rise to the top. And though not mentoring is quite different from actively undermining, both may operate from the same position of fear. And neither benefits the cause of workplace equality."[56]

Jocelyn Wright of The American College is familiar with the "Queen Bee" mentality in our industry. Here is her observation:

> We have to create a culture where women don't adopt that "Queen Bee" personality. Because there are so few women in our industry, sometimes women think there is no room for other women to come in and be successful, that in some way another woman's presence is going to take away from their position. We have to make sure that we are cultivating the sense that there is enough room for everyone. The pie is big enough for everyone, and if it is not, then we will just make another pie.
>
> I hear rumblings sometimes, with people saying, "There are just a few of us in the office, but she is doing very well, and she doesn't have time for me." Some

---

56   Peggy Drexler, "Can Women Succeed without a Mentor?" March 4, 2014, *Forbes* website, http://www. forbes.com/sites/peggydrexler/2014/03/04/can-women-succeed-without-a-mentor/.

women get the sense that maybe a female doesn't want to be helpful because it might take away from her shine. So we have to make sure that women are supporting women because it would be a shame if we got more women in management and didn't see them supporting other women.

As we are doing all of this, we have to make sure that we create a sense of sisterhood. This Madeline Albright saying has become quite popular in the last year or so: "There is a special place in hell for women who don't support other women." In industries like ours, that is particularly important. It is not always convenient to look out for someone or to make sure that another woman is doing okay, but we have to take that time and do that. It could be just as simple as a periodic check-in, but it makes a difference. You may be reaching out at the point where this young woman may think, "This industry isn't for me, and I need to go somewhere else." Your call just to say, "How is everything going? Hang in there. It gets better" could be all the difference that a young woman needs to decide she will keep going.

> *As we are doing all of this, we have to make sure that we create a sense of sisterhood.*

I was fortunate because when I started out in the business, I was very blessed to go into a firm or a practice that was owned by a woman who was extremely supportive of me. I appreciate so much her taking a chance on me and being supportive and mentoring me. As with a child, those first six years are the development years. Those were the first five years of my career, and her support was so important. I say all the time that I know I would not be in the business if it were not for Cheryl. I would not be here anymore because there were tough times when I thought, "It has to be easier somewhere else. I am just going to go get a job somewhere and be the Employee of the Month, instead of going through the struggle to start my own practice."

When we encounter a saboteur who wants to derail our success, we have to figure out if we are going to work around her or go over her. Getting the work done is the priority. Of course we want to do it in a friendly, collegiate environment where everybody likes each other. But if that doesn't happen, then we need to step outside of our environment and find a woman who can and will support us.

We can tell our new female hires, "Not everyone is going to love you or be invested in your personal success. Go look for those who are." The sooner women realize that, the better off they will be. Knowing this reality can help them avoid disappointment and discourage them from giving this kind of unfortunate friction more attention than it deserves.

Because women are reluctant to ask for mentoring, we, as leaders, need to look for opportunities to pair more experienced advisors with newer advisors. We also need to encourage our more experienced agents or advisors to reach out to other women in the industry and offer to be mentors.

At State Farm, offering to be a mentor to another person in the company was part of a manager's individual development process. This type of activity became check-offs that managers would submit to upper management. We (Thomasina and colleagues) wanted upper management to see that we were willing to extend ourselves and reach out to other women.

This is another area where the big "why" is critical. It is easy for all of us to say we are too busy to mentor another female in our industry. But if I am a female manager or veteran agent, my future is tied to the future of our newer female agents. The more women we help become successful, the better we will all be. The studies are consistent in showing that the mentors get just as much fulfillment as the mentees do.

> *The more women we help become successful, the better we will all be.*

Again, it doesn't always have to be a full-blown mentorship. Women can offer one another encouragement on a less structured basis—through an encouraging e-mail, a text, or a phone call. We can recognize a woman's accomplishment or acknowledge that she is going through a challenging time with family issues. We might know of an agent who just had a baby, for example. We can reach out to her and say, "I know this can be a challenging time, and I want to make sure you know that a lot of us have been through this. Here are some hints...and is there anything I can help you with?"

Provide Coaching for Women

Life coaching is a service offered by some companies and consultants. Coaching provides valuable one-on-one guidance that can be highly effective for women who want to build specific skills.

Jocelyn Wright shares this insight about the value of coaching:

> In coaching, we have to teach women to be advocates for themselves, speak up more, take their place at the table, and recognize that they should be there. The book *Lean In* talks about the "imposter syndrome," where you think you are not qualified for the position you are in. We need to help women have a greater sense of confidence. At times I still struggle with this. In the beginning of my career, I wanted to get as many designations as I could before even going out and talking to my first client. Fortunately, I had a mentor who helped me get past myself. We need to stop feeling like we have to know everything before we feel that we can go out and confidently talk to a high-net-worth client about a certain strategy or product.

Encourage Women to Be Loyal to One Another

We have mentioned the unfortunate situation in which women either fail to support other women or blatantly undermine their authority and derail their success. As leaders, it is our job is to foster a sense of loyalty and support in our organizations. Here are some thoughts from Lily Fong about the importance of loyalty in supporting women:

There are several ways a woman manager can help woman producers, to give a little lift of power or energy to your fellow women.

> *We can help each other by getting big cases and shorten the time to close a case.*

We can help each other by getting big cases and shortening the time to close a case. Recently, a man and I were talking about a woman from China who was an MDRT-level producer. He told me, "Yeah, she's an MDRT producer. But all her cases are small. She doesn't know how to do the big cases. She thinks it is too much for the client to pay for. She will shop around and get the cheapest product for the client, but not the right product for the client, because of her mind-set."

Women are so caring. We care about others more than we care about ourselves, and that is the problem. Men don't think that way. Men see it as, "The bigger the better. Who cares about next year? Let's just get this done." So the thinking is different.

We need more senior executives who are women. I met one recently who heads up a large company's diversity and inclusion division. She is very approachable and down to earth. She comes in, talks with everybody, and wants to learn and be included. It is easy to be loyal to a leader like that.

I think the sense of loyalty is very crucial in today's work environment. I see that many in the younger generation want to shortcut everything. They don't have a sense of job loyalty, they don't have loyalty to their supervisors or respect for their supervisors. If the younger women don't stand up and help each other, it is going to get worse because the sense of loyalty is not there like it is with our generation.

Once the loyalty is established, I think women should be more comfortable in helping other women grow. They just need to not be afraid that the younger women behind them will stab them in the back.

If something happens between men, they will shake hands and go play golf together. But women are mad at each other, day and night. How stupid is that? The men have a brotherhood. Why can't we have a sisterhood? We can help each other.

Surround New Hires with Positive People

When you are raising children, if you don't put them in association with other positive children, they tend to associate with kids who are not positive. I (Thomasina) think our situation is a little like being on the playground. If you don't get the women in your firm or agency around other women (and men) who feel good about what they are doing and who are trying to learn, grow, and do their very best, they may end up in the coffee room with the disgruntled people who are complaining about not being happy and not doing well.

As leaders, we need to be intentional about helping our female new hires surround themselves with positive, upbeat, successful, high-performing people. Everyone wins in this scenario.

Urge Women to Ask for Help

In Chapter 8, we discussed how many women think they have to be Superwoman and be the best at every role they play in their lives. Let's pull the veil back from the reality that if a woman works outside of the home, that doesn't exempt her from the work she needs to do inside the home. We need for women to understand that it is okay to get domestic help. It is okay to take the "S" for "Superwoman" off their chests. We cannot be phenomenal everywhere.

As female managers, we can help the women in our firms and agencies by telling them it's okay to say, "I can't do this; I need help." We need to educate females about the importance of conserving their mental and physical energy for the work that has the biggest impact. And that may not be cleaning out the refrigerator.

Women not asking for help is symptomatic of how we are socialized to be the caregivers who help others instead of accepting help for ourselves.

I (Linda) knew of a female agent who was a wonderful young woman and very committed to both her family and her career. She would take time off of work because she insisted on making homemade cupcakes for her child's school. I think that is really marvelous, but you can't be everything to everyone, and something has to give. Maybe it is okay to buy cupcakes from the grocery store or ask a neighbor/grandparent/friend to help out in this situation.

A veteran female manager in our industry tells a great story about having to travel for work a lot, and she felt bad about the fact that her husband and children wouldn't have home-cooked meals for the entire week she was gone. So she went to a lot of trouble and spent a lot of time cooking a variety of meals before she left. She labeled them and put them in the refrigerator and freezer. When she got back home, every last one of those meals was still untouched. Her family considered her being out of town as a vacation from eating at home and an opportunity to eat out. And they had a great time.

> *Her family considered her being out of town as a vacation from eating at home and an opportunity to eat out.*

Sometimes we do things for other people because we want to be caregivers, and it creates unnecessary and unhealthy dependencies that we don't realize. We end up teaching other people to depend on us to do things they could easily—and should—do for themselves. This is where you see the college roommate who can't make up a bed because she never had to; her mother did it for her for eighteen years.

It's about figuring out a balance. If we can find the answer for women, then we will get the answer for everybody. We all want to perform at a high level. We all want to get the job done, but we also want to have a life. How do you do both? It's our job as managers to help people figure that out.

Stop the Self-Defeating Colloquialisms

When we ask for help, we should not apologize for doing so. As female managers, let's remind other women of that.

It is really hard for some women to accept help graciously. One time, I (Thomasina) was mentoring a new manager who was having some problems getting her agents to perform. So we sat down and started talking. Everything I said to her, she would respond with, "I know, I know, I know."

I said, "I don't think I need to tell you anything anymore; you know it all."

She wasn't aware of how offensive that was to me in the position I was in, trying to help her. Again, we women need to help other women in this area and point out this type of self-defeating communication when we hear it.

Be Our Authentic Selves

> Sometimes women think they have to use a masculine communication style to be taken seriously. That makes things worse, not better.

Also, as mentioned earlier, sometimes women think they have to use a masculine communication style to be taken seriously. That makes things worse, not better. When we see our female colleagues doing that, we need to point it out.

Trying to be your authentic self as a woman in a male-dominated industry is an interesting sort of balancing act. We are not all alike, just like men are not all alike, so we need to encourage one another to be our authentic selves. We don't need to try to be like another woman or like the men in our leadership positions. We need to have confidence in our own strengths and recognize the value that we, as individuals, bring to the firm or agency.

Suggest That Women Ask for Feedback

As women, we should ask others whose opinions we respect for constructive feedback on our interactions with others. This is another type of informal mentoring or coaching. We can ask someone we respect to sit in on our conference call or presentation and provide us with constructive feedback. We should always try to improve ourselves without waiting for other people to offer suggestions.

The Kinder Brothers have said that you have to remain "a student of the game." We do that by constantly having the intellectual curiosity to learn more and ask for feedback. That is how we can grow as women leaders.

Conduct Self-Assessments

One of the things that was always helpful for me (Linda) was to give all new agents self-evaluation tests to help them get to know themselves better. We found the Kolbe Corp (http://www.kolbe.com/) evaluations to be effective. Instead of revealing your weaknesses, the Kolbe indexes reveal your strengths and how to leverage them. They have other indexes that help determine where people fit into a team best and help solve team productivity problems.

Another effective tool is the Gallup StrengthsFinder®. This assessment also reveals people's strengths and helps managers coach individuals to optimize those strengths (https://www.gallupstrengthscenter.com/).

Know Your Learning Style

In Chapter 5, we discussed the importance of knowing one another's learning style because it can be beneficial to our learning process. The three main learning styles are visual, auditory, and tactile (or kinesthetic). If I learn best through auditory media, then listening to podcasts of educational material will be effective for me. If I am a visual learner, then educational videos or books will be ideal. If I am a tactile or kinesthetic learner, then I need to actively engage in the learning process. In that case, writing or typing notes in a workshop or seminar will help me learn and retain the information.

As leaders, we have a better chance of engaging more people if our presentations contain all three elements. For example, instead of just showing a PowerPoint presentation to a group, we can embed relevant video clips into the presentation and provide handouts for people to use for taking notes.

To find out your primary learning style, go to www.educationplanner.org/ and answer the twenty questions.

Recognize Companies That Support Women

One way to encourage companies to focus on the well-being of women is to recognize those companies that are getting it right. In 2015, *Fortune* magazine released its inaugural list of "100 Best Workplaces for Women." Rankings were determined by employee surveys and the representation of women within the organizations listed.

A small wealth-management firm named TrueWealth made it to the number one spot. Based in Atlanta, the company has only twenty-six employees, and more than half (54 percent) are women. Even more remarkable, 67 percent of the company's managerial positions are filled by women, as are 44 percent of the executive positions. The perks include eighty-four days of paid maternity leave, flexible scheduling, telecommuting options, and twenty-six days of paid time off, including holidays and vacation days. There's also a focus on fitness: all employees are given a choice of a FitBit (an activity-tracking band that you wear on your body) or free health coaching.[57]

The perks include eighty-four days of paid maternity leave, flexible scheduling, telecommuting options, and twenty-six days of paid time off.

Recruit, Recruit, Recruit

Because recruiting is the heart of our business, it is every leader's responsibility to focus on recruiting. If we want the industry to attract more women, we all can be part of the change. Instead of saying, "Nobody else is recruiting women—how terrible," we can find women within our own networks and encourage them to consider a career as an advisor.

---

57 "100 Best Workplaces for Women," 2015, *Fortune* website, http://fortune.com/best-workplaces-for-women/.

Questions to Ask Yourself

1. Have you ever participated in a mentoring relationship, either as a mentor or as a mentee? If so, you can use that experience to establish a mentoring program in your firm or agency. If you have no female managers or veteran agents, consider helping your new female advisors find mentors outside your agency, or even outside the industry.

2. Have you ever used, or do you now use, self-assessment tools to help your advisors and managers discover their strengths? If not, consider the tools offered by companies like Kolbe Corp and Gallup. Knowing everyone's strengths will help you form effective teams and optimize everyone's potential.

3. Do you know what your own primary learning style is? If not, go to www.educationplanner.org/ and answer the twenty questions. Then have everyone in your firm or agency do the same, and record the results. This information can help you present training in a way that will ensure optimum engagement and retention.

4. When you hear or see managers or advisors speaking or acting in a way that does not project a positive self-image, do you mention it to them? (Privately, of course.) If not, you are missing opportunities to help people improve their interpersonal skills. It must be done delicately and from a position of genuine concern, but it can help increase people's awareness about habits they probably don't know they have. This is important because those habits could be barriers to a woman's ability to be promoted.

CHAPTER 11

A Vision for Our Industry That Can Change the World

"When we don't have to talk about it [gender diversity], the battle has been won."

—Jennifer Tory, Group Head,
Personal & Commercial Banking,
Royal Bank of Canada[58]

Despite the many studies that have proven the economic and social benefits of achieving gender diversity in organizations—and the general consensus that it is the best and right thing to do—we do not see the progress we thought would happen by now in our industry.

So what, exactly, do we hope to see?

A Balanced Workforce by 2020

We agree that the end game should be that the true American marketplace is reflected in the employment stats of our agencies, firms, and companies. We realize that it will happen incrementally, but there is no reason why we should not expect to have 50 percent of our advisors be females by the year 2020.

Our vision is that by 2020, the lack of women in our industry will no longer be a problem, and people won't need to read this book. We would like for the culture and the look of our industry to change so much in this area that we make a huge impact on society and the communities we care about. In this vision, the industry we love is a diverse and comfortable place for all people to be part of, and it is reflective of the marketplace, enabling us to help more people achieve financial security.

It has been my (Thomasina's) experience in business that people don't meet nice, should-have goals. They meet hard and fast goals. We all need to set specific goals and then chart ourselves against those goals every year. Then I think we will see real action. If we continue on this slow walk of increasing the number of women in our organizations by a few small percentage points every year for the next ten years, what will happen to our industry? We will not be equipped to serve the growing number of people who need help with their financial security.

---

58 "Women in Financial Services—From Evolution to Revolution: The Time Is Now," Oliver Wyman website, http://www.oliverwyman.com/insights/publications/2014/dec/women-in-financial-services.html#.Vih-Ck2sOSN4.

Americans Are Struggling

A lot of financial advisors in our industry are facing a crisis because they want to talk only with the wealthy, while the middle class is underserved.

We are seeing new studies about how we need to serve the middle market. Well, all of our insurance companies started out working with the middle market. Why is it now considered something special? If we don't respond to Americans' need for financial advice, our industry will get further and further away from our communities, and there will not be enough advisors out there talking to people.

Every three years, the Federal Reserve conducts its Survey of Consumer Finances. The 2013 report revealed that "substantial disparities in the evolution of income and net worth" have occurred since 2010. This is true despite the fact that the unemployment rate fell, and economic growth rebounded, following the 2007–09 recession.

The following facts from that government report show us that Americans are struggling, and the income equality gap is widening:

- The median net worth of American families tumbled during the recession years. Although the situation has stabilized, families haven't regained their lost ground.

- The gap between the richest and poorest Americans widened even as the US economic recovery gained traction in the years after the recession. The top 3 percent of Americans held 54.4 percent of all wealth in 2013, up from 44.8 percent in 1989. The bottom 90 percent held 24.7 percent of wealth last year, down from 33.2 percent in 1989.

- Average, or mean, pretax income for the wealthiest 10 percent of US families rose 10 percent in 2013 from 2010, but families in the bottom 40 percent saw their average inflation-adjusted income decline over that period.

- Take-home pay has changed little for middle- and upper-middle-class families, who failed to recover the losses experienced between 2007 and 2010.

- Only 65.2 percent of families owned their primary residence in 2013, the lowest homeownership rate since 1995.

- The share of families owning a business fell to 11.7 percent, the lowest level recorded in the survey's twenty-five-year history.[59]

To help Americans thrive again, we need diverse teams of financial advisors who mirror the communities they serve.

---

59 Ben Leubsdorf, "Fed: Gap between Rich, Poor Americans Widened during Recovery," September 4, 2014, *The Wall Street Journal* website, http://www.wsj.com/articles/fed-gap-between-rich-poor-americans-widened-during-recovery-1409853628 The Federal Reserve's 2013 Survey of Consumer Finances is available at http://www.federalreserve.gov/econresdata/scf/scfindex.htm.

From Scarcity to Generosity

In Chapter 1, we discussed how the overwhelming empirical data from numerous studies, along with our overall purpose, give us a compelling "why" for trying to achieve gender diversity in this industry. We want to help more people achieve financial security.

Thrivent Financial conducted a study quite a few years ago that talked about the ability our industry has to move people from financial *scarcity*—barely having enough to get by—to financial *generosity*. When people are financially secure, they can make a huge difference in their communities because not only are they secure personally, but they have enough financial security that they can share with others. Our industry can make a significant difference in the world if we help our clients move through that continuum, from scarcity, being barely able to survive, all the way to security, and ultimately to generosity.

Scarcity   ➔   Security   ➔   Generosity

That is the kind of vision we can have for our world. We all can make a significant difference, regardless of our politics. We love this industry. It has been not only our careers but our passion for decades, and we want a magnificent future—not just for ourselves or for the industry, but for the people we serve.

Better Service Can Reduce the Threat of Further Regulation

We do not know what the future holds, but in many countries, government regulations have made it more difficult for financial advisors to provide customized service to their clients. In some countries, financial advisors now are limited to providing more general solutions from corporate call centers, where individual advice is not given. We do not want to see this increase.

Government regulations already dictate and impact how our practices are run. One of the reasons the regulatory environment is becoming so onerous is that many consumers think our industry is not always operating in their best interest. If we build more and stronger relationships with our clients, we will have more clients standing up for the industry instead. That is where women can make a huge difference. Women matter because we have the ability to form deep personal relationships with our clients. With our more relationship-oriented perspective, we can help smooth out any regulatory and other outside influences that might impact our industry in the coming years.

> *Women matter because we have the ability to form deep personal relationships with our clients.*

And while we're on the subject—when leaders in our industry are at the table negotiating with regulators, how different would those negotiations be if more women were involved?

Years ago, I (Linda) saw research saying that although Americans had negative opinions of insurance agents in general, most had favorable opinions about their own agents, if they had a good working relationship with them. This information may be outdated, but it shows that people who have a relationship with a personal advisor don't have negative views of our industry. So if we build more personal relationships with clients—which, again, women excel at—we really can change the world. We can collectively increase consumer confidence in what we do and reduce the perceived need for regulators to intervene in the process.

In 2015, Deloitte surveyed two hundred executives at banking, securities, insurance, and investment management firms around the world. The researchers concluded, "What we learned is that firms are quietly transforming their businesses in anticipation of new entrants and disruptive trends. Their response to regulation is both pragmatic and optimistic. They're adopting new ways to attract and keep the best of a twenty-first-century workforce." One key to success in the future is what the report calls "human capital strategy." Ninety percent of the executives said talent retention will be a key to success, and 85 percent said having the "right skills in the right location" will be a key strategy.[60]

> *We believe gender diversity is the solution to having a larger, more capable pool of financial advisors available to help more clients become financially secure in a less regulated environment.*

We believe gender diversity is the solution to having a larger, more capable pool of financial advisors available to help more clients become financially secure in a less regulated environment. We think that having a more diverse workforce can also increase the retention rate among advisors in our firms and agencies.

Industry leader Charlie Reed sees progress already. She says, "We have the opportunity to really make a difference for those women who come after us. People are ready, for the first time in the lifetime of this business, to really hear it and act on it. It is very exciting."

The Future Is Up to Us

In a thought-provoking article titled "The Financial Services Industry in 2030," Matt Lynch, a Managing Partner for a financial services consulting firm, poses two different scenarios for the future of our business.

In the first scenario, which is clearly the ideal, Lynch imagines the following:

> Financial advisors now provide a more comprehensive spectrum of services that demand customization, including help with life-planning decisions. Trusted advisors become stewards of their clients' goals as well as their wealth. Transparency is essential regarding fees and other charges, as well as explanations of risk/reward trade-offs. A fiduciary standard is the norm, and consumers are more active participants in the planning and investment process. Financial advisors and the aided do-it-yourself channel reach collaborative leverage, ultimately benefiting the client.
>
> More women and minorities are entering the profession, thanks to company programs designed to provide mentoring, interactions with senior leadership, specialized training, and networking opportunities. These advisors are leading the

---

60 "Staying Ahead of the Pack: How Financial Services Firms Are Planning to Win," 2015, Deloitte website, http://www2.deloitte.com/global/en/pages/financial-services/articles/staying-ahead-of-the-pack.html.

way with financial education for clients and with interactive educational financial literacy games for upcoming generations. Women's communications and relationship skills and ability to address business and personal needs fit the evolving life-planning model. Additionally, women are better at bridging the trust gap; very few women advisors have been involved in the numerous financial scandals of recent decades.[61]

Women are better at bridging the trust gap; very few women advisors have been involved in the numerous financial scandals of recent decades.

In the second scenario, Lynch imagines a less-favorable reality in 2030:

> The industry continues to be perceived negatively by consumers because of continued financial services industry stumbles, and the trust gap widens. As a result, investors move increasingly to a self-service model to the exclusion of advisors and major financial institutions. Without professional input and encouragement, fewer investors take action to develop and implement long-term plans; others make poor decisions. Either situation jeopardizes long-term financial security.
>
> The industry maintains a status quo mentality and fails to develop programs to support the next generation of advisors and clients, including women and minorities. Advisors do not address increasing racial and cultural diversity, resulting in underserved markets and again driving investors to the self-service model.[62]

Of course we all hope the first scenario is the one that comes to fruition. And we hope you will be one of the leaders in making giant steps toward this effort. The sooner we all get started, the sooner we can reach gender equality, and the sooner we can make a positive impact in the lives of millions of American families. Let's change the world. Let's acknowledge that women matter—and do something about it.

Questions to Ask Yourself

1. By what year do you think it is realistic to expect that half of our industry's pool of advisors are women? What about half of your own workforce?

2. To what extent do you think having a more diverse workforce—one that mirrors your community—can help more people get the financial advice they need?

3. How motivated and committed are you to take giant steps toward achieving gender diversity in your firm or agency? When will you get started, and how?

---

61   Matt Lynch, "The Financial Services Industry in 2030," October 31, 2013, WealthManagement website, http://wealthmanagement.com/viewpoints/financial-services-industry-2030.
62   Ibid.

CHAPTER 12

The Importance of Support from the Top Leaders

"Never give up because that is just the place in time where the tide will turn."

—Harriet Beecher Stowe

Any initiative you undertake, especially one that is going to change the way your organization has always done things, requires unwavering support and guidance from the top levels of your firm, agency, or company. When you embark on your journey to achieve gender diversity, your messages all need to be clear, consistent, and communicated often—from the reasons you are doing it to your timeline to the steps you plan to take to get there. The message you communicate must be the same message your recruiter, trainer, sales managers, and everyone else communicate.

The roles and responsibilities of everyone in the organization need to be clear as well. Specify the expectations you have for your managers, advisors, and support staff in terms of recruiting, training, development, retention, recognition and every other process in your organization.

Diane Dixon, owner of 3F Coaching, says there are six critical success factors that must occur if you really want to change the demographics of your sales force. These are important whether you are a Managing Partner who is thinking about your territory or a home office executive who is looking at it from a corporate standpoint.

1. **Be the senior-level champion.** If you are the Managing Partner, you can't delegate this to your recruiter; you have to be the champion. Your recruiter can help you, and so can some of your trainers. But you have to be the champion of this effort, or it won't have the buy-in with the rest of your agency or firm and community. And if it is a corporate focus or initiative, it certainly won't have buy-in across the company unless senior executives at the highest level are the champions. When I was in Milwaukee, our two most senior leaders were my sponsors. We had great success while I was there because we had senior champions.

    > *If you are the Managing Partner, you can't delegate this to your recruiter; you have to be the champion.*

2. **Know and communicate your business reason for recruiting women.** Explain the reasons you are trying to increase the number of women you hire, why it is a good thing, and how you need everyone's help. That business reason needs to

be clear, and the message must be consistent throughout the organization. What the Managing Partner is telling everyone should be the same message that comes from your recruiter and trainer. What they are saying in the marketing department needs to be said in recruiting, training, and leadership development, and it needs to be said in the senior-executive-level meetings.

3. **Identify your cornerstones.** It is not about having a "fire sale" and getting a lot of women to join the company. It doesn't do us any good if we make hasty hires and the women end up leaving. Diane has identified four cornerstones. You need all of them; otherwise, your effort will be lopsided, and it is not going to stay long-term.

   a. **Promote women into leadership.** You have to shorten the leadership appointment curve because as it is now, it can take twenty years to appoint an agency leader. Could we please get a little more creative here?

   b. **Recruit more women.** Have a vision, and be intentional in your efforts. What are the recruiting tools you need, and can you do a recruiting blitz? What is some of the language you might need help with? Which women in your sphere of influence can be advocates for your vision and the career?

Which women in your sphere of influence can be advocates for your vision and the career?

   c. **Retain women and advance their productivity.** It is not just about recruiting women; it is really about retaining and advancing them. Ask them what they need and want.

   d. **Sell and provide service to women as consumers.** Make sure all of your marketing and planning tools and resources, as well as your strategies, include women as valuable and prominent consumers.

4. **Be strategic.** You can't just roll out programs; they have to be tied to a larger strategy. If you are a Managing Partner, this initiative needs to be tied to your overall business strategy, and it needs to be one of the key elements you are zeroing in on if you really want long-term success. For the corporate office, it has to be tied in at the very highest level.

5. **Provide adequate budget dollars.** When a company's leaders are serious about change, they put real money behind it. They don't throw token budget dollars at it; they put real money behind it, and they will hopefully have some nontraditional ways of doing things. Usually the company and the field are being asked to do some things differently and to take some different kinds of risk. This will require extra dollars, and we have to be willing to put them there, at the Managing Partner level or at the corporate level.

6. **Have adequate people resources.** If you are the Managing Partner, this doesn't mean just the people in your agency or firm; identify the people in the community you could build a relationship with and who could help you with this. Do you need a think tank from your community to help you do a better job with this? Corporate-wide, if you say, "This is a part of our strategy; we want to do this," but you do not put dollars and people behind it, it is almost a joke to your field force.

A Case Study about Building a Women's Initiative

Stacy Nystrom, a partner with Thrivent Financial, worked in Thrivent's corporate office for sixteen years. While there, she started a successful Women's Field Strategy to enable women to be successful in this career. This description of her experience provides us with valuable insight into how to start a new initiative to support women:

> Working in Thrivent's corporate office for sixteen years, I worked alongside our investment managers with our investment products. I served as a liaison between our investment products at Thrivent and our field force. That is where I developed relationships with the advisors and got to know our top-level producers. After being in that role for about ten years, I was ready for a change.
>
> Around that time, some of our top female producers invited me to their study group. I saw how effective the group was at getting together to share ideas and support each other. There is something unique about the different challenges women face, especially in this business. So I basically created a role for myself in what we call the Women's Field Strategy.
>
> My role with that strategy was to try to figure how to recruit more women and help them to be successful through mentorship and other types of support. That was the role that I was in for two years prior to transitioning to this leadership role. I got to be close with a lot of our females in leadership when I was in the Women's Field Strategy role, and that actually is what encouraged and propelled me to take the risk in becoming a field leader.
>
> When I was in the Women's Field Strategy role, I discovered that what didn't work was trying a whole bunch of things. I think you need to be very targeted about what you're going to try and then test that out to see if it is scalable and if you can implement it across the board.
>
> The most important thing I learned from female producers is that this can be a very lonely business, so it is very important for there to be a robust network of women in the business that you can connect with, whether it is a mentorship program or a study group. It is really important to have connections with other women in the region and across your organization. It can feel very isolating at times. We need to support women at different stages of their lives, whether they are raising young children or are empty nesters. We can provide opportunities for women to connect with one another and share ideas, even if they are not formal groups.
>
> When you host events, you have to have good content and good speakers. At the corporate level, I think we often forget that our advisors really want to share ideas. Frankly, the best ideas come from the advisors, and they really want to have time to share with each other instead of having the corporate office tell them what they should do. I facilitated a breakout session at a women's retreat, and I selected three of our

It is very important for there to be a robust network of women in the business that you can connect with, whether it is a mentorship program or a study group.

top women advisors and put them at different tables. Then I let the women who were attending hear their perspectives. You can't discount the opportunity for advisors to learn from each other.

In all of my roles, listening has been key. Listen to what the advisors are struggling with, then try to figure out what they need, whether it is to match them with someone else or to host a women's retreat or some other event so they can get together and share ideas with other women.

What really got me excited about making the change from the corporate office to a field leadership role was the fact that some other women were in leadership, and I saw that we had some similar qualities. I saw them in a similar role and I told myself, "I think this is something I can do." A lot of women need to hear, "You can do this" and "I think you would be really good at this; I see these qualities in you."

Based on this personal experience, Stacy also says top-level leadership must recognize that results might not be apparent soon. But it is important to stay committed to the initiative and be willing to wait for the valuable positive outcome:

> *We have to realize that it is going to take some time for the results to come; they are not going to be instant.*

We have to realize that it is going to take some time for the results to come; they are not going to be instant. And if you are really committed to helping women succeed, you are going to have to put some resources behind it. You cannot put a price on women feeling supported.

You can't try something for a year or two and expect things to change. It is going to take time.

We tend to look for results in production, but we need to consider retention too. Providing support to women in the field, creating a nurturing environment, will improve the skills of women who are new in the business, and it will help us retain them. Then the hard numbers will come.

At times, I encountered pushback from top leaders, and it was hard. I felt like I was the one person trying to move a boulder up a hill. I wondered how I could make an impact in helping women succeed—to make conference, for example.

I also got pushback from other producers. They asked, "Why are you doing something special for women? Isn't that reverse discrimination?" But we stayed firm and decided that we were going to continue to recruit and support women until our field force looked like the population in our marketplace—50 percent men and 50 percent women.

I think Thrivent is making inroads in launching women. About 25 percent of the new people we bring into the business are females.

The women's study group retreat that I started six years ago is still being held every year, and more women than ever are attending. About fifty women attended in the beginning; now about one hundred attend. Now it includes newer advisors as well. When we started it, it was for conference-level producers, which is our basic measure of production at Thrivent. I think the newer advisors need it more because it helps them get to know the top producers and learn best practices from them. We have women who are very willing to share their successes and their struggles, and that helps bring other women along. I think it helps with retention as well.

The retreat contains about two full days of content. In addition to having the attendees share their own ideas, I think it is important to spend money on an outside speaker as well. Having an accomplished woman come in to speak can be really helpful because then you are hearing a different perspective. Choose someone who has built a successful business, and ask her to share how she built her business, what her revenue looks like, and what works and doesn't work.

Also, when advisors hear an idea, they want to know how to execute it, how to get from point A to point B. They want to know the details about how to get it done.

You need to have buy-in from your top female producers too. At Thrivent, we have several top women producers who were sick of being some of the only women at the Pinnacle Leaders' Conference, which is our top conference level. They decided they wanted to help other women make it to the top. So we connected those high-performing women with women who had the potential to be successful but needed to be lifted up a little bit.

> *When advisors hear an idea, they want to know how to execute it, how to get from point A to point B.*

Emily Viner of Guardian is quite familiar with that feeling of frustration Stacy described:

There are days when I feel like I can't keep going because it is so hard. On my white board, I have a Harriet Beecher Stowe quote that says, "Never give up because that is just the place in time where the tide will turn."

What keeps Emily going is that she is beginning to see results from her efforts:

In the past couple of years, we have moved five women into first-line management, or on the path toward it. We have taken the time to nurture women. I am coaching a number of women, and we are getting close to 25 percent of women each year in our management training program. I can see the difference that our efforts are making.

And the woman who runs one of our offices in Albany now has reached the 50 percent mark—half of the people in her agency are women. She also has attracted a lot of Millennials. More and more of our offices are seeing these results as leaders invest in cultivating cultures where everyone can succeed. It might seem silly to say, but I celebrate the fact that we have lines for the ladies' room at training meetings now; it shows the shift on the front line.

Recognize and Address Women's Resistance to Sales Careers

Emily Viner says that in a 2015 Guardian study[63], the company found personal, culture, and career perceptions all contribute to stifling women's interest in a sales career. The research results show where the social norms and women's career expectations collide. Here is Emily's description of the five barriers:

1. **Women choose humility over hubris.** That is not say that all great salespeople have hubris, but ultimately, many women fear that they don't have the ego-driven personality to succeed in sales—but who wants a pushy salesperson, right? So there is this interesting dynamic—it is almost a reality check. Think of your most satisfying experience as a consumer; is that something you could do for a living? We've had several successful women join our firms who started as clients. After going through the planning process, they thought, "I could do what this advisor is doing. I can ask questions, listen to people, and come back with solutions to solve their concerns." If we challenge women to reflect on this, I think more would realize the opportunities that sales can present across any industry.

> *We've had several successful women join our firms who started as clients.*

2. **Women stifle their inner swagger.** The study revealed that 72 percent of women say they can lead their teams to success at work; however, women rank being a leader eleventh among their top traits. So women pull back and downplay a lot of their skills. We heard this in the GAMA Foundation research on recruiting top talent as well. Women are more likely to attribute success or their best qualities as those relating to helping and working with others. At some point, though, we need to own our individual skills and not fear showing those off too.

3. **For many women, inertia feels safer than risk.** Half of the women we surveyed are more comfortable sticking to their routine, even if it is not the best thing. They play it safe. That is not news to anyone; we know some women are a little more risk-averse about working on a commission basis.

4. **Women are navigating the workforce without a career map.** This is true particularly among women who are re-entering the workforce or looking to change careers. They don't have a leader to guide them along the way. This is more than simply holding up your CEO or top advisor; women want to see the path they need to take to get there. What does a career change look like six months, a year, or three years in? Mentorship and coaching are critical from a company and agency perspective. At Guardian, we encourage both women and men to seek out mentors and to become mentors. The key reason women leave any situation, whether in our business or in any other, is that they don't feel valued. The big accounting firms learned that fifteen years ago, when women said they were leaving for work/life balance, it wasn't really true. They were jumping to other firms because they didn't feel valued. We

---

63 "Closing the Gender Gap in Sales: Identifying Barriers and Redefining Career Options," Guardian, September 2015.

can get at the heart of this issue by offering coaching and mentoring, in addition to the other programs in place.

5. **Women feel pressure to be perfect.** Eighty percent of women set the bar very high for themselves professionally, and 70 percent of respondents indicated that they would always be stressed and under pressure in a sales job. This is a huge misperception, and I do not know where the disconnect is on this topic. It may come back down to having open, honest conversations about what the path to success looks like and not simply holding up an example of a woman who "has it all."

Emily says top-level leaders can address these barriers to entry by leading women to gain education and confidence:

So how do we help women overcome these barriers to sales professions? Education is one solution. Another is to continue to share how important it is to have a passion in this career. My mother became a widow at age forty-two. We had not done any financial planning nor had any insurance. We all know individuals who have come into this business because of personal experience. People who understand the impact of what we do have that passion. I would argue that passion gives many of us the swagger and conviction it takes to succeed. It takes sales out of the conversation because you're having meaningful conversations to help people.

> *I think that many women spend all of their time being competent, and they forget to be confident.*

Swagger is also tied to confidence. I think that many women spend all of their time being competent, and they forget to be confident. In this business, whether you are a male or a female, you need confidence, grit, and resilience. We need to educate both males and females about this. People who lack confidence in their ability and who do not have passion or grit face an uphill battle.

We obviously believe gender diversity is the key to serving our communities more thoroughly and to increasing revenue for every organization that embraces it. We see the gender gap in the insurance and financial services industry as a huge opportunity to increase the number of women we hire and promote. We look forward to seeing significant progress toward gender diversity in the next few years.

Questions to Ask Yourself

1. Given the importance of gender diversity, what do you think top-level leaders in agencies, firms, and companies need to do to attract more women into this industry?

2. To what extent can you personally drive a gender-diversity initiative in your organization?

3. What will be your first step in making gender diversity a priority? When will you begin?

Interviews the Authors Conducted with Industry Leaders at LAMP 2015

1. Do you recruit differently for women than you do for men?

Sherry Bogus, Branch Sales Manager, Bankers Life & Casualty Co., Houston, Texas

We have a slight change in emphasis. The first step is a group interview, and in the second interview, we tailor the discussion to what is important to the candidate, thus changing for whatever is important to the female candidate.

Sheri Cooper, CLF FIC CLTC, Managing Partner, Thrivent Financial, Fargo, North Dakota

Regarding recruiting and selection, don't judge a book by its cover. I started in this career with two young children. One was four, and the other was a year and a half, and I was pregnant with twins. Many people would have dismissed me as a candidate, but never underestimate personal determination and drive. I had family support because my husband and my mother- and father-in-law were all reps. Now I recruit women because I am a strong role model, and I can tell my story.

Ed Deutschlander, CLU CLF, CEO, North Star Resource Group; Mary Anne Smith, Second Vice President, Securian Financial Network; Diane (Dee) Yohn, CLU RHU FLMI CLF, Executive Vice President, North Star Resource Group; and Davin J. Bell, Financial Advisor, North Star Resource Group, Minneapolis, Minnesota

Mary: Our focus may be slightly different. For example, one of our Managing Partners tones down the forceful and competitive nature of the career.

Dee: For Millennials and for women, we lead our discussion with the impact one makes in the world.

Ed: We also talk about women who are successful in this career and about "life blend."

Mary: We have a Women's Group within the company that enables women to share experiences among firms.

Ed, Davin: It is essential for both men and women to judge a candidate's financial readiness. We discuss the time spent to start up the career and the impact of financial fluctuations in income.

Davin: During selection, it is important to ask "What is important to you?"

Herman Dixon, M.B.A., CLU CLF CPC ELI-MP, Energy Leadership Business Coach, Speaker, and Trainer, Charleston, South Carolina

I don't recruit differently for women than I do for men normally. I try to recruit to the position. I want to get the best person possible, so there's no difference in how you go about it. I don't look at whether someone is male or female; I look at the most qualified person for the opportunity.

Sandra Hughes, M.B.A., ChFC CLU, Agency Management, State Farm Insurance Companies, Madison, Wisconsin

Yes, I found that you have to look for female prospects more intentionally than males. Other male advisors will be quick to give referral prospects and/or associate themselves with males who could potentially be advisors. Males sometimes seek out the role; females do not.

2. Where have you had the most success recruiting women?

Sherry Bogus, Branch Sales Manager, Bankers Life & Casualty Co., Houston, Texas

Warm sources—referral bonus program for agents; community referrals, digital sources such as Monster.com. We don't specifically ask for women candidates. We do emphasize the opportunity to be a trailblazer during the recruiting process. It is important to find a few trailblazer females to "turn the corner." At first, one could leverage other agencies where women are top reps.

Ed Deutschlander, CLU CLF, CEO, North Star Resource Group; Mary Anne Smith, Second Vice President, Securian Financial Network; Diane (Dee) Yohn, CLU RHU FLMI CLF, Executive Vice President, North Star Resource Group; and Davin J. Bell, Financial Advisor, North Star Resource Group, Minneapolis, Minnesota

We have recruited most of our women off of the college campus. For the past five years, a woman has been either our number one or number two new advisor. Another excellent source for our women hires has been referrals from existing advisors, team members, and other community members who know our brand, success rate, culture, and reputation.

Herman Dixon, M.B.A., CLU CLF CPC ELI-MP, Energy Leadership Business Coach, Speaker, and Trainer, Charleston, South Carolina

My best source is referrals from my existing female agents, and the second thing I did was attend a women's symposium. I have to understand and know that female agents may not be able to really look at successors, or have someone to discuss their setbacks with anyone else but you, their manager. I had to understand they may have a lot of bouncing balls in the air. I found that it in a lot of cases, Mother Nature keeps women from being aggressive with someone they know. I've got to understand and work with their nature that has been ingrained in women since they were born.

Chris Gibbons, CFP FIC, Partner, Thrivent Financial, Philadelphia, Pennsylvania

Four of the women in my unit are high performing. For all, this is their second career, and all were recruited by referral from an experienced rep. Some have family members who are already in this career. One started in the unit as a community relations specialist. The second advisor moved from an established practice in another company. The third was a CPA and well connected in the rural Amish country. The fourth had prior experience in the company as a recruiter and in PR and corporate service.

Sandra Hughes, M.B.A., ChFC CLU, Agency Management, State Farm Insurance Companies, Madison, Wisconsin

I had most success in finding females from business groups (BNI, Rotary, small-business associations). My most successful advisors have been the females who worked in positions with the title of leader, yet they were doing all of the leading (coaching employees, making decisions, holding people accountable, etc.).

Henrietta Nye, Owner of Keir Educational Services; Coach; Trainer, Cincinnati, Ohio

We do most of our recruiting from CareerBuilder online services. We have had good luck with the quality of the applicants from that site.

3. Do you coach, manage, or lead men differently than you do women? If so, how?

Ed Deutschlander, CLU CLF, CEO, North Star Resource Group; Mary Anne Smith, Second Vice President, Securian Financial Network; Diane (Dee) Yohn, CLU RHU FLMI CLF, Executive Vice President, North Star Resource Group; and Davin J. Bell, Financial Advisor, North Star Resource Group, Minneapolis, Minnesota

Mary: It is important that women agents feel supported and valued if we are to retain them. If they are performing under Club level, they do not feel valued; however, they may exhibit good persistency in their business and demonstrate good client service. We also need to keep in mind that a woman's definition of success may be different than a man's.

Dee: We host small cottage meetings tailored to women for selling within their network.

Mary: The company has a support network for women with conference meetings and phone calls. For many, the only role models are men. Younger women need reassurance that it is okay to be themselves and not emulate the male model. They need successful female role models.

Ed: For a twenty-nine-year old female agent, our company helped her get donations to her high school to position her well in her community. This is a good example of helping women network.

Sandra Hughes, M.B.A., ChFC CLU, Agency Management, State Farm Insurance Companies, Madison, Wisconsin

Each individual is unique; I coach to the skills, desire, and talents of the person, regardless of gender.

Henrietta Nye, Owner of Keir Educational Services; Coach; Trainer, Cincinnati, Ohio

I believe I coach, manage, or lead each person in our operation in a different way. It is very similar to my parenting style—my kids accused me of not being fair because I handled them differently. That was the best way to get the results I needed. I hope I take each individual employee's needs into consideration when working with them and use the approach that will make that person the best that he or she can be. I am not aware of special styles I use for female versus male.

4. Have you identified any differences in training and developing men vs. women?

Sheri Cooper, CLF FIC CLTC, Managing Partner, Thrivent Financial, Fargo, North Dakota

Many women don't understand the role of selling, and I have to call this out. One new female recruit said, "I don't want to appear pushy and try to sell people something." I help women find a style that works for them, and most importantly, women need to see "selling" as helping others reach their goals.

Ed Deutschlander, CLU CLF, CEO, North Star Resource Group; Mary Anne Smith, Second Vice President, Securian Financial Network; Diane (Dee) Yohn, CLU RHU FLMI CLF, Executive Vice President, North Star Resource Group; and Davin J. Bell, Financial Advisor, North Star Resource Group, Minneapolis, Minnesota

Dee: While it is hard work to start, advisors have control over their time, which is appealing to Millennials and women. We help them think of another way to start the career instead of the traditional way. One example is that the firm can pay a candidate to start servicing orphan clients to get started.

Davin: One challenge is that we must be careful of eroding our culture due to part-time work.

Dee: Yes, we still use performance metrics. One thought for this challenge is to form a separate division for part-time work.

Mary: In the past, we have known only one way to enter the career. Internships are useful for both male and female candidates.

Davin: Sometimes a candidate can start by being a rainmaker for an experienced rep.

Herman Dixon, M.B.A., CLU CLF CPC ELI-MP
Energy Leadership Business Coach, Speaker, and Trainer, Charleston, South Carolina

Women are much more detailed, so you have to be prepared. Men often want to run on the seat of their pants. Women find that's not always the best avenue, that they want details. They want to find out the ins and outs and the nitty-gritty of the situation, which in most cases helps them really dig in and be more knowledgeable of the products and processes. Men often put their practical skills to work and then go back and make changes, so that's a big difference.

Sandra Hughes, M.B.A., ChFC CLU, Agency Management, State Farm Insurance Companies, Madison, Wisconsin

Yes, men tend to be more fearless...they just jump in and try it! I have found that females need to know more information, the reasons why, and the potential outcome.

Henrietta Nye, Owner of Keir Educational Services; Coach; Trainer, Cincinnati, Ohio

I am gradually learning that men and women want different information and amounts of information in presentations. I have not fully adapted my training yet, but I am trying to ask participants if the message or training is getting across.

5. What modification have you been forced to embrace to ensure gender diversity?

Sherry Bogus, Branch Sales Manager, Bankers Life & Casualty Co., Houston, Texas

About three years ago, our company started an initiative that was mostly women, and it resulted in a lot of male "bashing." Now our focus is on developing women, not trying to help men understand. The new focus is on development of women as a business driver, which will help all of us become more productive. The reason for this change came about because the committee working on this initiative became open-minded instead of combative. It was aimed at helping, was open to critical feedback, and made specific recommendations in stages. Now each geographic region has a woman liaison to the committee. Men serve on this Women's Initiative committee as well. For example, our recruiting emphasis was on money and flexibility of schedule. Now it is on making a difference and fulfilling a need in the marketplace, with less focus on flexibility and getting paid for your efforts. Our next step is developing a checklist for making one's agency more gender-diverse. If an office expresses an interest in this initiative, the manager will get this checklist with five categories to observe the following:

- How are your sales meetings conducted? Brow-beating in harsh tones or positive, with good critical feedback?

- Are schedules flexible for family commitments? Can agents work from home? Is the manager a role model for a balanced life, or does the manager work twenty-four hours a day, which is not attractive for women considering a management role?

- Are sales incentives all built around sports or sporting events?

- Do you encourage an informal support network? Is the culture inclusive and inviting, or is it more like a "cigar bar"?

- How do you talk with women agents about a management career? Do you encourage women to consider management opportunities?

Henrietta Nye, Owner of Keir Educational Services; Coach; Trainer, Cincinnati, Ohio

I have been looking at my presentation style and asking participants if they are getting enough or too much information. We are constantly asking our staff for "focused feedback" to help improve our meetings and training sessions. I think this is helping us to meet the needs of all participants.

Herman Dixon, M.B.A., CLU CLF CPC ELI-MP, Energy Leadership Business Coach, Speaker, and Trainer, Charleston, South Carolina

I think that with women, things are addressed in a more broad-based manner than with men because when a woman goes into household to talk to someone, she has concerns about their needs. She can more readily put herself in those seats to open up those donut-hole top areas with a little more respect.

Sandra Hughes, M.B.A., ChFC CLU, Agency Management, State Farm Insurance Companies, Madison, Wisconsin

A diverse team brings diverse thoughts. If the team is diverse, decisions will be challenged, additional ideas will be brought forth, and the team members will be empowered to participate. Women can naturally bring the care factor with feeling that someone is going to judge, whereas a male is not as comfortable in expressing the care factor.

Henrietta Nye, Owner of Keir Educational Services; Coach; Trainer, Cincinnati, Ohio

You need the sales team to have both men and women because your clients are both men and women. This will help you to be more sensitive to the interests and needs of the clients. The variety of gender, ethnic backgrounds, and any other differentiators will help bring a variety of ideas to your organization. The variety of advisors should help to attract a variety of clients.

7. What one or two strategies/ideas have you implemented that led to improved gender diversity in your firm or agency?

Sherry Bogus, Branch Sales Manager, Bankers Life & Casualty Co., Houston, Texas

Keeping a focus on the business case and the bottom line. There is a strong need in the marketplace for serving women clients. This has a consistent long-term focus for our company. One of our leading male managers has been vocal in his testimony about the positive impact of having women in his agency. His comments have created much support. We also have a quarterly Best Practices Teleconference to share gender-diversity strategies. Having men on the committee has been helpful. There is also a Women's Leadership bimonthly newsletter with tips on creating gender diversity.

Sheri Cooper, CLF FIC CLTC, Managing Partner, Thrivent Financial, Fargo, North Dakota

Another important aspect of gender diversity is having women on the leadership team for the region. My regional leadership is 50 percent female. This helps tremendously with recruiting and supporting women agents.

Sandra Hughes, M.B.A., ChFC CLU, Agency Management, State Farm Insurance Companies, Madison, Wisconsin

Meet with female advisors monthly. Have them share what's going well, lessons learned, and solutions for challenges as an avenue to create a community for support.

8. Where do you think gender is in your operation and the industry now? Is it an issue?

Sherry Bogus, Branch Sales Manager, Bankers Life & Casualty Co., Houston, Texas

Compared to ten years ago (Sherry started in 2001), there is much improvement, and there is still much to be done. About 37 percent of our Unit Field Trainers are female, and 6 percent of our Branch Sales managers are female. The challenge here is that this position requires one to relocate, and females have often been burdened by a husband who will not/cannot relocate. The Millennials are changing this, however, because young men tend to be open to relocating to help further their wives' careers.

Ed Deutschlander, CLU CLF, CEO, North Star Resource Group; Mary Anne Smith, Second Vice President, Securian Financial Network; Diane (Dee) Yohn, CLU RHU FLMI CLF, Executive Vice President, North Star Resource Group; and Davin J. Bell, Financial Advisor, North Star Resource Group, Minneapolis, Minnesota

Ed: Today, 47 percent of our new starts are women, so we are making some headway. We have found that during college-campus recruiting, the Millennials have a more open mind-set about career choices.

Henrietta Nye, Owner of Keir Educational Services; Coach; Trainer, Cincinnati, Ohio

There is still a preponderance of men in the insurance industry. From what I see in the research, women would prefer to work with women, so I would have to say yes, this is an issue. If a firm has a variety of advisors, you would expect to have a greater variety of clients.

R. Michael Condrey, CFP CLU ChFC CASL, Managing Partner; and Dee Condrey, Recruiter, Northwestern Mutual, Raleigh, North Carolina

The number one challenge in our organization is that of a "white-male culture." We have a challenge to just being aware of this fact. Our new CEO has a fifteen-year road map for the organization, which is stated as "White Men as Full Diversity Partners." We are focusing on eight key leadership skills. Part of the challenge of having a white-male culture is the attitude of the white male agents themselves. So even if a manager is working toward gender diversity, the current male agents are often resistant to this change.

Our number two challenge is that our statistics show that men and women don't succeed at the same rate. Women agents often don't stay, so we have a retention issue. And when we do exit interviews, these women say they don't feel like they fit in. So a male manager has to publically and privately stop the white-male "banter." Male managers have to lead by example. When it comes to recruiting females, we have to work simultaneously on culture and sourcing. We need to source where top females are. And we need to have a culture in which women will be comfortable and feel like they fit in and are valued.

9. How does this compare to ten years ago?

Henrietta Nye, Owner of Keir Educational Services; Coach; Trainer, Cincinnati, Ohio

There are definitely more women in the industry than there were ten years ago. Firms are making a real effort to hire women.

10. How was it when you first came into the business, and how long ago was that?

Sherry Bogus, Branch Sales Manager, Bankers Life & Casualty Co., Houston, Texas

In 2001, I got into this business because I was attracted to the income potential and the opportunity to move up.

Sandra Hughes, M.B.A., ChFC CLU, Agency Management, State Farm Insurance Companies, Madison, Wisconsin

When I came into this business twenty-five years ago, there were not many females in leadership or as independent business owners/advisors.

Henrietta Nye, Owner of Keir Educational Services; Coach; Trainer, Cincinnati, Ohio

I started in the business thirty-two years ago. It is dramatically different! Women unfortunately did not see the great opportunity for this career. The flexibility of hours is perfect for women raising children.

11. Where do you see it going in the next ten years?

Sandra Hughes, M.B.A., ChFC CLU, Agency Management, State Farm Insurance Companies, Madison, Wisconsin

The same, unless we learn to approach female prospects differently.

Henrietta Nye, Owner of Keir Educational Services; Coach; Trainer, Cincinnati, Ohio

I believe we will see more and more women entering the financial services industry. Because women live longer and seem to want women advisors, there will be more demand for women advisors. Women are more confident of their talents, and I believe they are more comfortable with a commission-based business. I do believe the starting positions will have more options than the traditional 100 percent commission situations, and possibly paraplanner positions to allow women to test the waters with more secure income. As companies get more creative with the compensation packages, I believe more people (not just women) will consider the financial services careers.

12. What suggestions can you offer?

Sherry Bogus, Branch Sales Manager, Bankers Life & Casualty Co., Houston, Texas

It needs to continue to improve, and companies need to continue this focus at every single company event. This consistency will create much-needed change.

Sandra Hughes, M.B.A., ChFC CLU, Agency Management, State Farm Insurance Companies, Madison, Wisconsin

We need to hear or read the success stories of female advisors in these areas:

- Balance (family, business, community)
- Emotion (guilt, support, self-care)
- Financial freedom (travel, assets, legacy)
- Development (leadership, coaching, business planning)

13. Do you think there should be a change?

Sandra Hughes, M.B.A., ChFC CLU, Agency Management, State Farm Insurance Companies, Madison, Wisconsin

Yes, the change must start with our mind-set. We must believe that by adding female advisors, we can accomplish the following:

- Better serve the customer and make stronger connections.
- Increase revenue.
- Bring other females into the industry.
- Create an improved work environment for everyone.
- Gain recognition for the organization as "a place for females."

Henrietta Nye, Owner of Keir Educational Services; Coach; Trainer, Cincinnati, Ohio

I think society benefits by having the industry more closely reflect the population. I am sure firms will look to hire Hispanics, Chinese, etc., in areas where these groups are in large numbers. Companies will always be looking for ways to better relate to the people, so it is a good thing to have a variety of advisors to relate to the people in local neighborhoods.

Suggested Resources

Bruce Christopher Seminars—Comedy with Content, http://www.bcseminars.com/.

Guardian Life Insurance Company of America. "Closing the Gender Gap in Sales: Identifying Barriers and Redefining Career Option." New York, September 2015.

GAMA Foundation for Education & Research. "Recruiting Women to the Advisor Career." Falls Church, Virginia, 2014.

GAMA International, www.gamaweb.com.

Jordan, Joe. "Living a Life of Significance: A Woman's Perspective." http://www.josephjordan.com/.

Kolbe Corp assessments and evaluations, http://www.kolbe.com/.

Million Dollar Round Table (MDRT) Mentoring Program, https://www.mdrt.org/membership/mentoring/.

Pink, Daniel H. *Drive: The Surprising Truth about What Motivates Us*, Kindle edition. New York: Riverhead Books/The Penguin Group, 2011.

Reed, Arthea, and Diane Dixon. *Financial Services: Women at the Top—A WIFS Research Study.* iUniverse, 2015.

Sandberg, Sheryl. *Lean In: Women, Work, and the Will to Lead.* New York: Knopf, 2013.

The American College State Farm Center for Women & Financial Services, http://womenscenter.theamericancollege.edu/primary-research#.

Women in Financial Services, https://wifsnational.org/.

About the Authors

Daralee Barbera, CFP CMFC CLF ChFC

With more than three decades of experience, Daralee entered the financial services industry in 1982.

Daralee holds a bachelor's degree in mathematics (summa cum laude), as well as a master of arts in secondary education from California State University, Long Beach. Daralee holds the designations of CFP (Certified Financial Planner), CLF (Chartered Leadership Fellow), ChFC (Chartered Financial Consultant), and CMFC (Chartered Mutual Funds Counselor).

Daralee was honored to be named the WIFS "2013 Woman of the Year." In 2013, she was also listed by LifeHealthPro as one of the "20 Women in Insurance You Need to Know."

She has been featured in the *Orange County Register, GAMA International Journal,* GAMA's "Great Ideas" series, National Underwriter, LifeHealthPro, *Advisor Today, The Wall Street Journal,* Business Wire, Yahoo! Finance, MarketWatch, *The Wealth Channel,* World News, *International Business Times, The Buffalo News, California Broker, Financial Planning, InvestmentNews,* and KPPC and KNX Radio in Los Angeles.

Daralee was the 2014–15 president of GAMA International Board of Directors. She also serves on the 2014–15 Board of Advisors of the Northwestern Mutual Granum Center for Financial Security at The American College. She will serve as a trustee for the American College starting in 2016. She is Chairman Emeritus of the Orange County Chapter of the FPA (Financial Planning Association), which is formerly the IAFP (International Association of Financial Planning). She is also a member of NAIFA (National Association of Insurance and Financial Advisors), Women in Film (executive member), and WIFS (Women in Insurance & Financial Services).

As an award-winning and well-decorated leader in the financial services industry, Daralee is also an internationally recognized speaker. She is coauthor of the books *What You Can Do...When You Can't* and *What You Can Do...When You Can't—21 Days to Personal Success: The Workbook.* These books encourage others to always do what they can do, even when they feel like they can't, with a clear twenty-one-day formula for goal attainment.

Daralee is a native to Los Angeles and lives in Manhattan Beach, California.

Thomasina E. Skipper, M.B.A., ChFC CLU CLF
Business Growth Specialist, Atlanta, Georgia
http://thomasinaskipper.com

Thomasina Skipper began her career with Fireman's Fund Insurance Company in Cleveland, Ohio, as a Personal Lines Underwriter. In 1981, she left Fireman's Fund to become the Vice President and General Manager of Citizen Insurance Agency, an independent insurance agency. That role led her to establish one of the first female-owned, independent insurance agencies in Tennessee.

In 1986, Thomasina joined State Farm Insurance Companies. In 1992, she was transferred and promoted to Atlanta, Georgia, as an agency manager. In 1995, Thomasina became the Agency Field Executive for the Metro West Agency Field Office in Atlanta, and she later transferred to Omaha, Nebraska. Thomasina retired from State Farm in 2013.

She holds a bachelor's degree in political science, with a minor in economics, from Syracuse University. In 2001, she earned her M.B.A. degree from Kennesaw State University in Georgia with honors.

Thomasina was a main-platform speaker at LAMP 2010, and she has made presentations to the sales-management staff at various companies in the industry. She is a member of the GAMA Speakers' Bureau and a visiting lecturer for The American College. She is a past member of the Board of Directors of GAMA International and of the GAMA Foundation, and she served as chairperson of the GAMA Women in Leadership Task Force. In 2008, Thomasina received the GAMA First in Class Award in Leadership, and in 2013, she was GAMA's Cy Pick Awardee. For twenty-two years, she qualified for State Farm's Ambassador Travel Program, and she was the company's 2010 Master Multiline Award Winner.

Thomasina and her husband, Benjamin Skipper, have four children and five grandchildren.

Linda L. Witham, CFP ChFC FIC
Owner, LLW Leadership Consulting, LLC
Ventura, California

Linda Witham spent twenty-eight years with Thrivent Financial. As a Managing Partner, she grew new middle-level leaders to achieve the overall growth of the Southwest region. Through the hiring and training of a diverse group of representatives, she led ten middle-level leaders to grow their zones.

She launched and led many successful marketing and change-management initiatives for Thrivent. From 1998 to 2011, the Southwest region was the top sales region nationally within Thrivent.

Linda made history in 2009 when she became the first female to become the president of GAMA International, an association that has served field leaders in the insurance and financial services industry for more than fifty years. She has chaired and served on numerous GAMA committees. Since 2011, she has served on GAMA's Women in Leadership Task Force. She was a main-platform speaker at LAMP in 1995 and 2010 and has been a motivational speaker at many additional industry meetings and conferences.

She received the GAMA Master Agency Award every year from 1998 to 2011. In 2010, she was named the WIFS Woman of the Year, and she received the Soaring Eagle Award from Kinder Brothers International.

In addition to her industry designations, Linda holds a BS degree in education from Concordia College in Seward, Nebraska, where she graduated summa cum laude.

Linda and her husband, David, reside in Ventura, California.

57178889R00089

Made in the USA
Charleston, SC
06 June 2016